THE GREATEST WELSH TRIES EVER

(Colorsport)

THE GREATEST
WELSH TRIES EVER

GERALD DAVIES

Gomer

Acknowledgements

The author and publishers wish to thank the following individuals and publishers for their respective permissions to reproduce some of the quotations used in this publication:

University of Wales Press for the extract on page 9; Robert Hale Ltd for the extract on page 13–14; Mainstream Publishing for the extract on page 19; The Orion Publishing Group and © The Trustees for the copyright of Dylan Thomas, 1945, for the extracts on pages 27 and 69 taken from *Collected Poems: Dylan Thomas*; Sioned O'Connor on behalf of the estate of Albert Evans-Jones ('Cynan') for the extract on page 89.

The publishers also wish to acknowledge the permission of the WRU to reproduce the photographs on pages 3, 12, 145, 146–7, 148–9.

Published in 2013 by
Gomer Press, Llandysul, Ceredigion, SA44 4JL

ISBN 978 1 84851 738 7

A CIP record for this title is available from the British Library

This book is published with the financial support of the
Welsh Books Council.

The publishers would also like to acknowledge the generous contributions made by
the Press Association and Colorsport to the publication of this book.

www.paimages.co.uk   www.colorsport.co.uk

Printed and bound in Wales at
Gomer Press, Llandysul, Ceredigion

CONTENTS

INTRODUCTION

For all the drama of the last-minute kick at goal, there is no sporting theatre as epic as the try in rugby football.

Whether it is the culmination of a grand, poetic, length-of-the-field movement, or the result of a relentless period of more prosaic pressure on the opposition line, nothing thrills like the touchdown. And this is as true on the school yard as it is on the great international stages, like the Millennium Stadium and Eden Park.

But there are tries and tries, and the greatest of these have become part of the collective consciousness of rugby folk the world over. And this is especially true in Wales where rugby remains a seminal part of our national lives. Think of a 19-year-old Keith Jarrett collecting a bouncing ball to run half the length of the field to score on his debut against England in 1967; of Gareth Edwards emerging from the mud against Scotland in 1972; of Ieuan Evans sidestepping the whole of Scotland in 1988. Who can forget Scott Gibbs making a corner of Wembley forever Wales in 1999, or Shane Williams twinkling his way to the try line in Pretoria in 2008?

Which is the greatest, however? In this book I have set myself not only the impossible task of selecting fifteen of the most memorable tries ever scored by the Welsh international team (with one enigmatic exception), but also of choosing from these the best of the best.

Such a selection is, of course, invidious; subjective, as such choices must be, they are sure to prompt disagreement and debate, in the best traditions of those rugby discussions which were part and parcel of Sundays in Llansaint, the village in Carmarthenshire where I was brought up.

Whether you agree or disagree, I hope you enjoy, as I have, revisiting these perenially epic theatres.

Gerald Davies
October 2013

BOB DEANS
v. WALES

National Stadium, Cardiff
16 December, 1905

'The Bob Deans incident was… vital for rugby history… It symbolized the continuing struggle for supremacy… the 'try' was the grit in the oyster that produced the black pearl for future generations.'

The Fields of Praise, Dai Smith and Gareth Williams

Wales's infatuation – no, let's not mince words – true passion for rugby union football began with a try, or rather a try that was not a try. This long-standing affair had an uneasy and bewildering beginning but, despite the uncertain foundation, Wales and rugby have subsequently shared a full and magnificent life together. Since 1905, if there have been ups and downs in the way the national team have played, good times and bad times, this passion has not diminished; a devotion, tender at times, obsessive the next, is vivid still.

In 1905 Wales played the New Zealand All Blacks in Cardiff and the tale of the 'try' began. The match proved to be the defining moment when the early flirtation became a lifetime's engagement. Wales had made swift progress at the end of the previous century and had won the first Triple Crown in 1893, during which time Arthur Gould

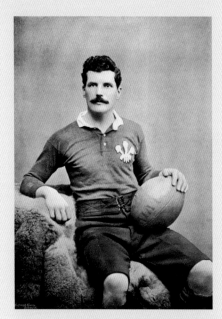

Newport's Arthur 'Monkey' Gould, forerunner of the modern-day rugby celebrity.

(Press Association)

created the forerunner of what was to become the modern-day rugby celebrity. He was a star attraction.

The new century ushered in what is now referred to as the first 'golden era' when Wales, with the advent of Frank Hancock's revolutionary four-man three-quarter line, were able to challenge the other three home countries on an equal basis. Their new tactical permutation was the way ahead and, as a result, scoring tries became more important.

Such progress prompted a surge of interest in the game in Wales, but what truly galvanised public support was the victory against the all-conquering All Blacks, led by Dave Gallaher. The tourists had played 32 fixtures conceding only seven tries, three of these in Wales. They were beaten only once: by a Wales team captained by Gwyn Nicholls. It shaped things to come.

Furthermore, the controversy and the legend that grew around whether Deans had scored or not scored a winning try proved to be of universal interest, and ensured that rugby in Wales would form a conspicuous part of the nation's culture and become rooted in the national psyche.

It all boiled down to the curious incident of 'the try', indicating the emotive importance of the touchdown in rugby, as much as its essential utilitarian value. Hitherto, after all, kicking goals had been the main manner of collecting points in rugby.

The choice of Deans's (disallowed) try may seem at odds with the purpose of this book: my personal selection of favourite Welsh international tries. However the impact of the 'try' on the development of the game in Wales was invaluable and established rugby as the country's national game.

Indeed, the match itself was described as 'the most fateful in the history of rugby football' and 'the world's championship in rugby'. The atmosphere was exceptional, as described in the consummate Welsh rugby history: Dai Smith and Gareth Williams's *The Fields of Praise*.

The scoreboard clicks on, or shifts digitally, to record the mathematics of the match, while down below on the fields of praise, we look on searching, not only as a fleeting day dream, but in our wistful longing for the game's greater good, for more than just a record of the accumulating scores. Of course, those figures matter: who's winning, who's losing; who's up, who's down. We want to know

The Welsh team which defeated New Zealand in 1905: (extreme back row) Linesman Ack Llewelyn; (back row, l-r) Tom Williams (WRFU), J.F. Williams, George Travers, Dd Jones, W. Joseph, Rhys Gabe, WRFU President Sir J.T.D. Llewelyn; (middle row, l-r) C.M. Pritchard, Jehoida Hodges, Willie Llewellyn, Gwyn Nicholls, Bert Winfield, Cliff Pritchard, A.F. Harding; (front row, l-r) Teddy Morgan, Dicky Owen, Percy Bush. (Press Association)

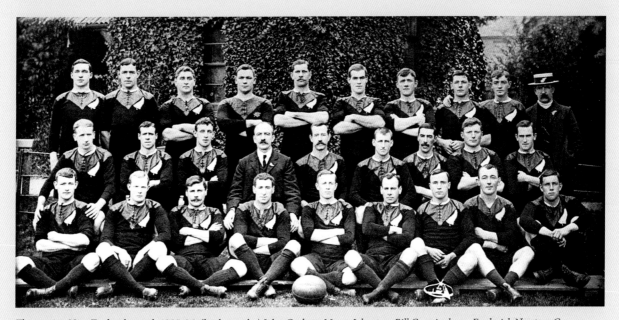

The touring New Zealand squad, 1905-06: (back row, l-r) John Corbett, Massa Johnston, Bill Cunningham, Frederick Newton, George Nicholson, Bronco Seeling, James O'Sullivan, Alex McDonald, Duncan McGregor, James Duncan; (middle row, l-r) Eric Harper, Billy Wallace, Billy Stead, manager George Dixon, captain Dave Gallaher, Jimmy Hunter, George Gillett, Frank Glasgow, William Mackrell; (front row, l-r) Steve Casey, Bunny Abbot, George Smith, Fred Roberts, Mona Thomson, Simon Mynott, Ernest Booth, George Tyler, Bob Deans.

(Press Association)

what our team did; or are doing. What's the score? is the fundamental question, after all. This is the reason why we watch, why we buy the ticket.

Ray Prosser, coach of the opponent-annihilating Pontypool teams of the 1970s and 1980s, would have agreed. An injudicious supporter once tapped him on the shoulder to commiserate with him when Pooler had lost by a single point to Cardiff: 'Not to worry, Pross. It's only a game…' The great man's retort said it all: 'If it's only a game, as you put it, why the 'ell do we bother keeping the score, then?'

This is elemental: narrow, possessive, tribal even, because team sport *is* tribal. We take sides.

But once this primary desire is satisfied, do we not go further in our enquiry? We, surely, want to know what lies behind the score. We are curious to know what kind of game it was and what our heroes

New Zealand captain Richie McCaw
is tackled by Gethin Jenkins and Leigh
Halfpenny at Cardiff in 2012.

(David Davies/PA Wire) © Welsh Rugby Union

did. We seek to know. Did our favourite player make his mark and, if so, how?

The bald facts of the score are there and will remain in the record books. We will refer to the statistics in years to come but they can only come alive if we recollect, even with failing memory, the exceptional moments when we were intoxicated by the dynamic sweep of passing and running, the brilliance of the singular man or of the unity of teamwork. This matters.

Rugby is more than what the formal account on the ledger and what the bare bottom line shows. We want to know how the figures emerged, the fine detail of the interesting events that led to the results. We want to know how Keith Jarrett amassed his 19 points against England in 1967. Such a total is fascinating especially if it is a nineteen-year-old boy just out of Monmouth School who gets them, all the while playing full-back for the first time ever.

This was by any estimation an extraordinary feat, but how much more extraordinary when we realise that, in amongst the kicks at goal, he ran with such youthful confidence for some 50 yards to score a glorious try. If earlier he had kicked his goals to immense cheers his try was greeted with thunderous, joyous applause. This, more than the kicks, satisfies what enhances our love of rugby football.

We bring our personality to bear on events, our emotions play their part. We want our vision stimulated, our imagination engaged. We want to live that time again for the sheer love of what rugby can exhilaratingly be and, more often than we care to think, actually is. The score matters, but matters more if there is a try in the count. But, for all that, we are repeatedly left passive and disconsolate because of the repetitive roll call of, quite often inexplicable, penalties.

In each match, at the whim it sometimes seems of the referee, whose forefinger ever so frequently points skywards, each team aims a penalty kick at the posts. The match progresses almost predictably with the chance of three points offered one way, then, after a suitable passage of time, three points the other. Frustratingly or jubilantly, depending on the choices the referee makes, the match marches on based on a succession of these kicks at goal. Its conclusion is the loser's anguish, a weariness of the spirit; a sense of disenchantment which seeps into the infatuated supporter who, like a jilted lover, is left with the overwhelming question: why?

We are left unclear as to why the whistle went and, if it did, why the penalty went the way it did? Even the winner's celebrations are ultimately unfulfilling since there is a lack of clarity as all are left to wonder about the discretion of the referee and the licence he has to interpret the Laws. This raises the suspicion, rightly or wrongly, of the influence he may appear consequently to have in determining the outcome of the match. This lack of clarity as, for example, in the discrepancy that used to exist between the scrum put-in law as it was once written and the referee's application of it, is manifest to all observers, compromising the well-being of the game, and risking a sense of betrayal.

Admittedly, the suspended animation of the attempt at goal provides suspense and drama in such a fast-moving game, but it is the scoring of a try that provides the delight and sense of the fun of the game. It is what gets us up on our feet. We are as a child again, unconfined.

Yet the penalty was in rugby's early days the point of it all. The touchdown meant that the team had a 'try' at goal. Here is the history:

> In the game's earliest beginnings, matches were decided purely by goals, a try or rouge or touchdown as they were then referred to, having no scoring significance unless it was converted into

a goal. Indeed the rouge or touchdown was looked upon merely as the opportunity to kick at goal. In 1875, however, the try did achieve something akin to recognition in that three touchdowns or rouges were adjudged as equal to a try, three tries in turn counted as one goal. It was not however until 1887 that the adoption of the rules at Cheltenham College saw the try accorded a definite numerical value. This was varied somewhat in 1889 when the Rugby Union decreed that the value of a penalty goal be reduced to two points but the ruling differed from that of the International Board's which affixed the scoring values for International matches as follows: goal from a try = 4 points, dropped goal or goal from mark = 3 points, try = 2 points, with the reservation that when a goal was kicked from a try only the goal counted.

The Encyclopaedia of Rugby Football
compiled by J.R. Jones (Hale, 1958)

What feelings might there have been among the 47,000 crowd – the largest for the time – who were there that afternoon on 16 December 1905? Not many spectators saw much of the game. Not everyone saw the 'incident'. If the day had opened to sunshine and clear skies, by kick-off time a thick mist had settled on the Arms Park and stayed there for the whole game.

Strictly Come Haka. It was at Cardiff in 1905 that the All Blacks performed their iconic Maori war dance for the first time. And they would perform it again against Scotland two weeks later. (Press Association)

The *haka* – 'not very musical' it was said 'but very impressive' – was performed for the first time on Welsh soil. To counteract this, Wales were going to sing '*Hen Wlad Fy Nhadau*', the national anthem, but which was listed fifth in the programme selection as a Welsh 'air' and would be sung after the haka. How would the modern-day New Zealand team react to their war dance not being top of the bill? When it was courteously requested by their Welsh hosts in 2006, Richie McCaw's All Blacks remained in their dressing room and performed it in private, like sullen adolescents, not having their way.

Wales's try that day was scored by Teddy Morgan, and, as it turned out, it was the game's only score. From the reports it was a good one and could well have counted in my choice in this book. Anyway, the conversion from an awkward angle failed. 3–0 to Wales.

Morgan 3 Deans 0! Wales's Teddy Morgan scored the only points of the game.

(Press Association)

With ten minutes remaining of the game, Wales, according to the reports of the day, were deserving of victory. Then the source of the controversy began.

It began as a counter attack from within New Zealand's half. Billy Wallace went through the Welsh defence, according to Messrs Smith and Williams, 'like a mackerel through a shoal of herrings'. Llewellyn tackled him as Wallace threw the ball to Bob Deans 30 yards out, halfway between posts and the corner flag. Deans turned inwards.

This is where the confusion begins as to whether Deans crossed the line, or instead whether he was brought down short of the line and, contrary to the laws, wriggled his way over before being pulled back. The reports are contradictory. Peering through the mist made overall judgement difficult. Llewellyn claims the tackle as does Rhys Gabe. John Dallas the referee disallowed the 'try'.

Sir Terry McLean wrote that the incident was the 'greatest event in the history of New Zealand rugby because it provided a basis, a starting point, a seed of nationalism upon which all aspects of the game were to depend in succeeding years'.

For Wales this famous game saw rugby tethered, moored and anchored in the Welsh national consciousness. Rugby union football became inseparably identified with Wales and New Zealand.

That it was a great game was not sufficient of itself to have this enormous historical impact; that there were great players in both teams attracted attention but was not enough; that it was played in front of the largest crowd hitherto and one which was in fervent

Bob Deans, non-scorer of the greatest try never scored. (Press Association)

partisan mood, singing 'Hen Wlad Fy Nhadau' for the first time might have hinted at something more than curiosity; that Cardiff was on song and Westgate Street closed to horse-drawn carriages; that the victory was at one with the progress of Wales's first 'golden era'; that it was given comprehensive journalistic coverage gave it prestige and magnified its importance.

That Wales won would have secured its fame and would ensure that it would be talked about. But that victory over time would be

A war dance on the world stage. New Zealand captain Wayne Shelford leads the haka before the 1987 Rugby World Cup semi-final against Wales at Ballymore, Brisbane.

(Colorsport / Colin Elsey)

rendered as a mere statistic, a score in the ledger along with so many others. The 'try' however took the game into another more exalted realm and transcends the conventional international match. The glimmer of that 'try' from within the heavy mist has radiated throughout the century. It has entered mythology. With such an exceptional influence how can it not be included amongst all the tries that were *actually* scored? This 'try' has a significance beyond all others.

1905 ———— BOB DEANS ————

KEN JONES
v. NEW ZEALAND

National Stadium, Cardiff
19 December, 1953

'Wales was the match that mattered.'
Keith Davies (All Black)

'We were aware of the history, and Billy Wallace, who had played in
1905, was still around…'
Bill Clark (All Black)

Dragons and All Blacks, Huw Richards

If 1905 is seen as a significant signpost in Welsh rugby's history and
the beginning of a special relationship between two rugby-loving
nations, this alignment of sporting interest was more than manifest
on a cold frosty day in December 1935, when seven tons of straw had
covered the pitch overnight to ensure a playable surface as Wales
prepared to beat Jack Manchester's Third All Blacks. It was further
crystallized with the visit of Bob Stuart's Fourth All Blacks in 1953,
Wales's last victory against New Zealand. And, once again at Cardiff
Arms Park, where the visitors had yet to win a game, a memorable try
was scored, this time by Ken Jones. Like Teddy Morgan's in 1905 and
Geoffrey Rees-Jones's in 1935, his also proved the winning score.

Unlike the other two tries, however, we could all bear witness to this one by Jones and can still do so to this day, over a half a century later, on the Movietone News.

Tries can be valued and celebrated for any number of reasons. There is the joy of the simplicity of the single but expert execution in a narrow field, say, when squeezing in and managing – just – with an intake of breath almost, to avoid the corner flag; or, open-jawed, to await the capricious bounce of the ball as it is delivered tantalisingly to the expectant open palms or, presuming nothing, the hopeful, outstretched fingers, dreading the worst, but, coming good, welcomed with a sigh and heavenwards-thanking eyes; or the anxiety and suspense of the lonely long-distant run to the line, like an episodic drama of what-happens-next, as the fugitive on the run is given hair-raising chase to his sanctuary. Or, and what is given the highest accolade, the heroic, multi-handed sweeping epic of rugby theatre reaching its apotheosis in *the* Barbarians try of 1973.

They all stay in the memory.

Which is where Ken Jones's try remains.

This one belongs because it begins almost in desperation.

New Zealand's Brian Fitzpatrick is held up as he tries to ground the ball at Cardiff in 1953. Ken Jones (no. 2) looks on. (Press Association)

Hook, line and sinker! Ken Jones scores at Twickenham in 1952 before England's William Hook can catch him.

(Press Association)

Ken Jones, born in Blaenavon, played rugby for West Monmouth Grammar School in Pontypool whence he emerged to win his Welsh Secondary Schools caps, appeared briefly for the town club before carving a distinguished reputation for himself on the wing for Newport. In a 12-year period for the club he scored 145 tries.

By all accounts, Jones, 5ft 11 inches and 12½ stone, should have collected a lot more, but isolated on the right wing, towards which side there is less of an inclination to move the ball – stuttering, heavy-handed, watchful and less instinctive – than there is to pass to the left – more innately sure, frictionless and with ease – Jones was left mostly in the cold. (Rugby's left-right skill-set contrast is equally apparent when we compare the well lubricated kick with the right foot and the inelegant attempt with the left.) Few can master the two sets of talents with equal agility and grace.

If he was left empty-handed – no doubt to grow, like all wingers, ruminative and philosophical – for Newport (scoring, for example, only six tries in 18 matches in 1951, when he captained the club in their championship year), he fared a little better for Wales. He scored 17 tries in what was then a world-record 44 appearances. 43 of these had been in succession, until he was dropped from the team to play England in 1957, only to return against Scotland in the next match!

He proved more prolific in New Zealand and Australia, where he scored 17 tries in 17 matches for the Lions in 1950.

But this is only part of the Ken Jones sporting story. He was seven times Welsh sprint champion over a 100 yards. He won an Olympic silver medal in the athletics relay in London in 1948, competed in the Empire Games in Vancouver 1954 and was made captain of the Great Britain team in Berne's European Games in the same year.

When the match against the All Blacks beckoned in 1953, Jones had not missed an international fixture since 1947.

Not unremarkably, there was also another Jones running the line that afternoon, one Ivor Jones.

Jones was a remarkable player, playing for Llanelli ('Llanelly' with a 'y' in his day) from 1922 to 1938, captaining the club for nine seasons and scoring, astonishingly, over 1,200 points in his career. They thought the world of him in New Zealand too: during the Lions tour of 1930, which included a visit to Australia (where in one game he scored 22 out of the 29 Lions points), he played in all five Tests. He scored the winning try in the first Test in New Zealand and scored in the third Test too.

In a land where back-row forwards are the kings of the game, New Zealand were happy to think of Jones as being of royal lineage. When he returned to that country in 1969 as President of the Welsh Rugby Union, he was instantly recognised among the All Black cognoscenti and celebrated for having made such an indelible mark 39 years earlier. The surprising point is that for all his Scarlet longevity and his great renown, the 'Big Five' selectors saw fit only to pick him 16 times for Wales. Indeed, he was never chosen again after he came home from that Lions tour. After he retired, he served 19 years on the WRU Committee from 1947, and was three years on the International Board. He became WRU President in 1969.

He was, as they say, a legendary figure, a man of considerable and unquestionable accomplishments who would, dare I say, not be slow

'Cross kick, Clem, cross kick.' Ivor Jones, great back-row forward and advisory touch judge, played his part in Ken Jones's famous try in 1953.

(Press Association)

in choosing to remind those in his company of them. And who knows, it may have been to secure his place in Welsh rugby's pantheon, to add further luminescence to his lustre, that he attached his name to the famous 1953 try at Cardiff Arms Park.

So it was that as Welsh wing-forward Clem Thomas ran towards the river end on the left side of the pitch that afternoon, the touch judge outside him was Ivor. Clem seemed caught in something of a quandary, not certain what he should do with the ball next. And that's when Ivor, according to Ivor, shouted to Clem: 'Cross kick, Clem, cross kick'. Which, of course, is what Clem famously and historically did. Whether this was part of Clem's imaginative quick thinking or intuition, or whether he heard Ivor's cunning plan and instruction above the Arms Park din, can no longer be verified. Both of the leading players in this drama have, sadly, departed the stage. But that was the tale as it was regaled to me by Ivor one evening in New Zealand where stories of his fabled deeds were legion.

The sequence began with Cliff Morgan seemingly looking for a half gap, changing his mind in a flash before putting in a low-trajectory kick towards the South Stand touchline. Gwyn Rowlands got there but Elsom of New Zealand hindered him and the ball went loose. Thomas got his hand to it very close to the touchline, underneath the watchful eyes of Ivor Jones in his flannel trousers and blazer. Thomas shaped to throw an overhead pass, hesitated, looked up and kicked into midfield. The bounce favoured Ken Jones who took the ball at speed and in one movement sidestepped the full-back under the posts.

It was a great moment in Welsh rugby history: that 13–8 win meant that Wales were now ahead by three games to one in their duels with New Zealand. It is a sobering thought for all Welshmen, however, that their country has failed ever since to triumph against them.

Large All Black 'Tiny' White is tackled by the creator of Ken Jones's try, Clem Thomas (no. 15). (Press Association)

Man and ball. New Zealand's Allan Elsom is about to feel the weight of Billy Williams's tackle. (Press Association)

1953

KEN JONES

Wales's Barry Williams (no. 2), Gwyn Jones and Scott Gibbs are outnumbered by Jonah Lomu at Wembley in 1997, as Josh Kronfeld (in scrum cap) looks on. New Zealand could have done with the great winger in Cardiff 44 years earlier.

(Colorsport)

Stuart Watkins: composed, balanced, unflappable.

(Colorsport)

STUART WATKINS v. FRANCE

National Stadium, Cardiff
26 March, 1966

'As I was young and easy under the apple boughs
About the lilting house and happy as the grass was green.'

'Fern Hill', Dylan Thomas

I am given to sentiment. This is not by way of an apology, as is so often the case with the male of the species, who hesitates to admit to a view coloured by emotion. Mine is merely an expression of fact.

What is sentiment but a warm attachment to a fond memory or a heartfelt acknowledgement, open and on show, of delight in what has been; or an affectionate, fellow feeling towards someone or something? Your heart is firmly on your sleeve, and it is a cold colleague – not a true companion with whom to share a moment – who cannot summon from within a similarly benevolent spirit and softness of mood. Too often this milk of human kindness is interpreted as vulnerable and schmaltzy. Its expression vulgar and lacking balance and reason. You read as much in newspaper columns.

It began with the death of Princess Diana when there was an outpouring of grief, which was criticised in some quarters.

But what is rugby without sentiment and affection. Were it not for the emotion we bring to the game, what appears in front of our eyes is but a series of shapeless scuffles. To the untrained eye, it is merely a chaos of bodies; of brutal collisions ending in graceless and clumsy heaps; only occasionally bursting out aesthetically into a thing of beauty and majesty.

I think of Stuart Watkins's try against France at the Arms Park. Seeing the Newport winger in full flight over 70 metres was surely a thing of beauty. He was tall for a winger in those days, something which might suggest all that is ungainly and maladroit, but Watkins was self-possession itself. He was composed, balanced, unflappable throughout, master of the moment. Majestic indeed. With stately progression, unaffected and smooth, he moved from deep, French defenders chasing him all the way. It was a heroic odyssey.

'Tall for a winger' Stuart Watkins (extreme right) stands firm with his Welsh forwards against France in 1966. They are, from left to right, Gary Protheroe, Norman Gale, Alun Pask, Bill Morris and Howard Norris, and they would later thank him for his match-winning try.

(Press Association)

I had not seen anything of the kind before. International tries were hard to come by. Long-distance ones were rarer still. You needed to go back to newsreels in the cinema to catch sight of Malcolm Thomas's long run in 1951 or Bryn Meredith in 1957. My recollection of Watkins's try might so easily have faded over time and his run not been quite as exhilarating as I remembered it. But the newsreel footage – the match was not televised – continues to confirm how thrilling it was.

Stuart Watkins had begun his international career in 1964. He joined what was a fairly well-established Welsh team. Alun Pask and Brian Price were exceptional forwards, talented and knowledgeable. Denzil Williams joined them along with Norman Gale who had been first capped in 1960. Dai Hayward and Gary Protheroe formed what was a complementary duo on the scrum's open and blind-side flanks: the one, from Cardiff, speedy and creative while the other, from Bridgend, tenacious and unbreakably hard-boiled. All the while, Haydn Morgan of Abertillery remained a challenger after his first cap in 1958. Grahame Hodgson was an immaculately correct full-back, doing everything that any standard coaching encyclopaedia advised.

In front of him D. Ken Jones, Adonis-like with flowing blond hair and sculpted physique, was the player I wished to be, as I had seen him from the 'tanner bank' at Stradey Park, Llanelli, scoring one of those daring tries that stay forever in the memory. It was against the Irish Wolfhounds very early in the season, where he ran from just inside his own half, sidestepping three people – oh, at least three! – in quick succession to dive over glamorously and spectacularly near the posts.

It was the kind of dashing try I wished for and thereafter dreamed of scoring. Did I not imitate, time and time again in the open field of the Parc y Tŷ in Llansaint, overlooking Cefn Sidan and Carmarthen Bay, that touch of mercurial magic and allure I had witnessed that mid-week evening after the cheerless and forbidding school day was over?

It was in the same manner as the try he scored in the first Test at Ellis Park, Johannesburg, for the Lions in 1962. Except in South Africa we only saw one of his superlative sidesteps and not the trio he administered so seamlessly and fluently that evening in September in Stradey. The Lions try was recorded, however, so I can still savour the flavour of Jones's great style as other memories fade.

'The player I wished to be': D. Ken Jones takes them on at Twickenham in 1966.

(Press Association)

It had the touch of chivalry in its daring and courage, and romance in its flamboyance and fancy. It stands apart among the game's rough and tumble ways. I hope I don't sound snobbish but it is the poetry among the prose. Each, the tough graft and the delicate art, is essential and have their place in the scheme of things.

In Wales's 1964 backline Dai Watkins occupied the hallowed no. 10 jersey. With his curly-topped head tilted back, as swift off the mark as a sprinter out of the blocks, he could dart and dash, skim and scurry over the best and the worst of surfaces – as he did against Scotland in 1966 to set up Ken Jones for a try.

Dewi Bebb was on the left wing. He had begun his rugby career at 21 years of age while a teaching student at Trinity College Carmarthen, and after three games with Swansea and a final trial match, he was chosen to play against England at the Arms Park in 1959. He scored a try on his debut, an unlikely one given the rain which pelted down on a treacherous fenland surface. But, with full-back Terry Davies converting from close to the touchline, it proved to be the winning score.

Overnight Bebb became a hero to us all: we were schoolboys, graduating from the joy and high jinks of the yard, ripening suddenly, primed for the grown-up promise of rugby and of its superior sporting status in Wales.

What we had heard from the local experts was true then, whether they were the village grand jury, cross armed and cross legged, idling the day away on the bench in the shadow of Llansaint's church tower, or the elders outside the chapel after Sunday's morning service, setting aside the sermon for chapter and verse on yesterday's match, or matches to come. Rugby was made to seem important in people's lives and significant on the national stage. Men talked about it a lot, and if the heat of the debate was on, they did so with finger-wagging gravity. It was solemn stuff.

We listened eagerly but only from a child's hip-high vantage point; to be seen was alright but certainly not to be heard. Adult talk is always tempting. You might even get to learn a new word or two.

'Now listen good boy, Brace is a fine scrum-half, no doubt about it. Oxford graduate and all that, and a Blue to boot,' a wag once pontificated. 'But what I say is, he's too unorthodox….'

'Unorthodox'? What could they mean? Was this good or bad? Could he kick and could he pass? That was the point surely?

Outside half David Watkins performs the cancan against England in 1966.

(Press Association)

'Unorthodox'? The dictionary was called for. And so we learnt about rugby and how to talk about it. Who's in, who's out and why. When I saw Onllwyn Brace again, I tried to fit the meaning of the strange-looking word to the action. It was true. He did things differently and questioned the conventional view.

And as Bebb inspired us at home watching the television, so his try inspired the crowd at the Arms Park. It was the first time I heard 'Hen Wlad Fy Nhadau' sung as the game came to a close. The best choir in the land, my father said, believing that the Morriston Orpheus Choir had been given free tickets to the North Stand so they could sing the Welsh team home.

Leading this talented group of players was 'Top Cat' himself, Clive Rowlands.

He played 14 times for Wales, each time with David Watkins as his partner at half back. Rowlands was made captain on his debut for Wales, the first since J.R. Evans in 1934 to be accorded that particular honour. There are those who claim that his personal style of playing was limited, but Rowlands played according to the laws of the game and the conditions at the time. Since nothing – no sentimental view of playing what might be thought a more 'attractive' game – would veer him away from following a simple, most effective route, to winning a match, then so be it.

He was as wily as they come, tactically astute and massively knowledgeable about Welsh rugby history. He managed a victory at Murrayfield in 1963 (where Wales had not won for ten years), from which success grew the improbable legend that he kicked the ball so often that 111 lines-out ensued in a period, would you believe, of 80 minutes? This was a Wooden Spoon year, the first since 1949, but the team was set on a trajectory which saw them share the Championship the following year while 1965 was a Triple Crown season. The loss against France that year signalled the end of Rowlands's international career.

'A hero to us all': Dewi Bebb dives over at Twickenham in 1964. (Press Association)

'Top Cat', top dog, top man: Triple Crown-winning captain Clive Rowlands is chaired from the pitch after victory over Ireland in 1965. (Press Association)

He was and continues to be a hugely influential figure within Welsh rugby. For me he was an inspirational coach. He was a great motivator and, ironically, while he played rugby in his singular minimalist style, he persuaded all those players who came under his influence as coach, to play an expansive game. He wished each player to express himself, generously. He gave us freedom.

Also his words and emotional manner echoed the comments of those men from my village who saw in rugby a firm unshakeable identity for Wales. Rowlands made us all aware of his strong belief in national consciousness, asked us to understand where we came from, where we belonged; who, in fact, we were. This was to be our inspiration.

With this in mind I have many times wondered how he would have made an extraordinary politician in the newly developing Welsh democracy. I knew his inspiring speeches before a Wales match, passionate and uncompromising. We are never to know what he might have been like, given a wider brief, in the Assembly chamber in Cardiff Bay. For sure, in his irascible way, there would be nothing moderate or lukewarm. There would be passion and, shall we say, perturbation in the house; a few feathers ruffled. What excitement and expectation there would be. And what oomph!

It was into his team that Stuart Watkins entered, but Rowlands would no longer be in favour in the spring of 1966 when Watkins seized the day against France. I was a reserve that day so I witnessed the try, not at a distance, but there from the North Stand of the Arms Park. I was there. This is also a reason why I have chosen this try. It was such a wonderful and intoxicating experience.

We need reminding how rare it was that tries should have been scored at all in those days. Penalties were the key factor in most games, which were low scoring by nature. The list of matches and the score lines during the period provides ample evidence of this. Such a colourfully dramatic try was unheard of, excepting Malcolm Phillips's sublime try for England on the frozen and hazardous Arms Park surface in 1963, the type of score which breathed rare life into frequently rather immobile contests. Indeed a year earlier these two teams had played out the drabbest of drab draws, 0–0!

By 1967, the law governing the kicking into touch had changed (as a result, so many believed, of Clive Rowlands's kicking demonstration at Murrayfield!). So when, under the new law, Wales played England in April sunshine, instead of the normal January, the scoring totals and margins changed: this was Jarrett's game and Wales won 34-21. High scores thereafter became commonplace.

When Watkins first intercepted the ball close to his own 25-yard line (as it then was), he must simply have been relieved that he had stemmed a threatening French attack. The River Taff end was not an immediate objective, not when he began his journey, but after realising how well he had done it must have suddenly dawned on him what potentially lay ahead. He looked up and, as if peering through the wrong end of the telescope, he realized he had a long way to go. Thankfully he did not consider kicking as an option. Had he done so, what drama we would have missed: a tantalizing journey deleted.

And so he pursued the advantage, did not let go, and went bravely and improbably in search of his journey's end. It was not a crowded field. It was an open space. Unless you have been there, you cannot truly understand the dilemma that this open space brings. It looks

The greatest Lions try ever? George North beats Will Genia's despairing dive to score against Australia during the first Test at Brisbane in June 2013. Stuart Watkins was considered a big winger in his day. What then of the 6 ft 4in, 17-stone North?

easy but this is an illusion. The line ahead may well be clear but who is behind me, or how many, and how fast are they encroaching on my space? Are they closing in? Am I running fast enough to avoid them? There is so much time to think. And to look back inhibits the running. It slows the runner down.

It so much better not to think. Well, not too much at any rate. Better to allow instinct to take over, as if the body itself knows how best to respond. And yet the mind, reacting however swiftly and briefly, must have ultimate control. Watkins had so much time to think and, by doing so, to worry and to ache, knowing that this was a great chance which was so near and yet so far. It was within his grasp to win the chase. But between cup and lip…

And so Watkins swerving in and out, fending off a would-be tackler, slightly hunched with long, loping strides, eating up the ground as a 400-metre runner would, bemusing Lacaze, the French full-back, reaches the line triumphantly. I can recall my enthusiasm still at the imperious sight.

STUART WATKINS

1966

'Slightly hunched with long, loping strides' Stuart Watkins has the line in his sights against Ireland at Cardiff in 1969, ushered by Keith Jarrett.

(Colorsport)

Keith Jarrett: the epitome of boldness.
(Colorsport)

Try 4

KEITH JARRETT
v. ENGLAND

National Stadium, Cardiff
15 April, 1967

'Bliss was it in that dawn to be alive,
To be young was very heaven.'

I remember writing these words from William Wordsworth's poem
'The Prelude' during the Rugby World Cup in New Zealand in 2011 as
they applied to the Wales team of that time.

They were a youthful team. George North on the wing was a
teenager, Scott Williams at centre was 20, as was Toby Faletau in the
back row. Two of the scrum halves, Lloyd Williams and Tavis Knoyle,
were 21. Sam Warburton at 22 was captain. And in their confident,
composed manner, they were a revelation, on and off the pitch.

The young respond boldly to the responsibility and pressure – if
they ever consider it as such – that is thrust upon them. They are
not yet fully acquainted with fear and are full of hope. Unlike the
careworn adults who have known suffering and adversity, they have
no sense of foreboding or trepidation: these young bloods absorb

Sam Warburton, youthful captain of the Welsh young bloods at the 2011 Rugby World Cup, sprints away to score against Fiji.

(Press Association)

new experience, they are not inhibited by it. Indeed, the only burdens upon them are those insinuated upon them by the so-called wisdom of the greybeards.

This is true I believe in all walks of life. When confronted with the prospect of appearing in front of a vast crowd and the sense of awesome challenge that lies ahead, the young player is proud that he or she has been called upon to be among the cherished few to wear the nation's jersey. He is inspired by the occasion not cowed by it. It is the honour of a dream fulfilled; what has been, until this moment, the stuff of far-fetched imaginings. He is doing what he always wanted to do; he is so happy to be there on his glad, confident morning.

In the Rugby World Cup in 2011 Wales's young tyros played superbly and earned the respect of their New Zealand hosts, as well as the admiration of those who watched them play. To be young was indeed very heaven.

Keith Jarrett was only four months out of Monmouth School when he appeared in the Welsh jersey on 8 April 1967. At 6 foot and 13 stone he was ideal for the centre position where he had played all his rugby hitherto. However, for his first international cap he was chosen at full-back where he had not played before.

At 18 years of age he was following in the footsteps of another schoolboy rugby protégé, Terry Price, who was also 18 when he played on the wing for Llanelli at Stradey Park against Wilson Whineray's All Blacks in 1963 and who, against England two years later, won the first of only eight caps. In those eight games he would amass 45 points. That he would prove such a prolific points scorer for Wales had been presaged in the final trial match, when he scored 16 points, including two tries from full-back.

All Blacks' captain Wilson Whineray, supported by Waka Nathan, gallops away to score against the Barbarians in 1964.

(Press Association)

Price had been a prodigious scorer as a schoolboy. He was a pupil of Llanelli Grammar, a school with an enormous rugby reputation bolstered by success on a national scale at the Rosslyn Park Sevens competition, which attracted participants from all over England. Llanelli were there by invitation after winning the equivalent Welsh schools sevens competition traditionally held in Llanelli over the Easter period.

Having played in that competition, I can vouch for Llanelli Grammar's expertise and dominance over several years, superbly coached as they were by their PE master Hywel Thomas who seemed, in his meticulous application of coaching principles, way ahead of his time. Llanelli were the aristocrats of the tournament. They lorded it over everyone else. And during the late 1950s and the beginning of the 1960s there was inevitability about their ultimate success.

Such success was a cause for celebration, but it would later become a burden.

Keith Jarrett in his Newport colours.

(Press Association)

In those far ago days the rugby authorities were hostile to the very thought of coaching, seeing it as a threat to the hallowed principle of the amateur ethos. Indeed, coaching in rugby did not become part of the mainstream in Wales until 1967 when Ray Williams was appointed Coaching Organiser of the Welsh Rugby Union. But it was often regarded with suspicion elsewhere. In Scotland, for instance, their first coach was not even officially recognised as such, posing instead as 'Advisor' to the captain, whilst on the 1966 Lions tour to New Zealand, John Robins was called the assistant manager even though he actually shouldered the coaching responsibilities. He was in other words the coach in all but name.

Having a coach smacked too much of 'professionalism' which word, damning as it was in an amateur sport, was soon applied to Llanelli Grammar School at Rosslyn Park in Roehampton and at less prestigious Oxfordshire sevens tournaments. Llanelli were certainly an expert team with expert players and won these tournaments almost at will, but what proved their nemesis had as much to do with the way they looked as their staggering success. They had, it seems, the audacity to parade between matches in uniform tracksuits bearing their school colours, suggesting a swagger which was not theirs by right.

They certainly did have something of a proud strut, the kind which would have looked more at home on the playing fields of the public schools of England than in a tinplate town in South Wales. With their all too efficient performances and corporate clothing, they were accused of professionalism and were not invited back again.

Those educators who outlawed Llanelli Grammar eschewed the thought of and the search for excellence in sport. They already seemed old. What was happening in the game was passing them by. They could not see or understand the changing spirit of the age.

It was the way things were.

Schoolboy or not, Terry Price had a rugby maturity beyond his age. Like a meteor dazzling brightly for a brief moment and then – not disciplined enough to subdue his wilful streak of independence, not wishing to be hidebound by authority but wanting to go as he pleased, however prodigal – he faded. Invited to join the Lions in New Zealand in 1966 he limped off the plane in Auckland to the mystified representatives of the New Zealand media. He was overweight and grossly unfit.

By 1967 he had gone 'north', as the phrase had it, to play for Barrow. It meant going to the north of England to play rugby league in Lancashire and Yorkshire.

The full-back position had suddenly been vacated without warning: it had been a position likely to be occupied, it seemed obvious, by Price for some time to come. Whatever his truant shortcomings he had established his international credentials rapidly, but Wales's failure to win a game throughout the Championship meant that Wales were heading for a 1967 whitewash. The final game was against England in Cardiff and they were coming for the Triple Crown. Price's poor form against France in Paris led to his exclusion. Where should the Big Five, as the selection committee was then called, go?

Terry Price, Jarrett's fellow schoolboy protégé, who also went 'north'.   (Press Association)

Remarkably, they went for a complete novice. They chose Keith Jarrett. Admittedly he had played with astounding success at Newport since leaving school in December 1966. He had scored 109 points in 16 games. But he had never played full-back. At the behest of the selectors Newport chose him there for their next fixture against Newbridge. It did not work out and not long into the game they returned him to the centre. It was too late for the Big Five to have a change of heart.

It was a high-risk strategy. It worked and in phenomenal and unforgettable fashion.

Wales won 32–21. Jarrett scored 19 points with five conversions and two penalties. But the pièce de résistance in all this was his try.

Wales were in command of the game. They were pressing close to England's line. Colin McFadyean, the England centre, put in what he thought would be a relieving kick. It was high but fell short of the ten-yard line.

As I was playing in the game, I did not notice until I later watched it on television what a remarkable intervention Jarrett's running was. The television picture of the pitch showed an empty space. The ball touched the ground and bounced high. This was April. Unlike the past when Wales used to play England in January when the conditions were invariably dark, damp and soggy underneath, the ground for this match was firm. The only other time the pitch had been this firm was when the frost had set in in 1963.

The ball is high. There is no one around and as the ball begins its downward trajectory suddenly Jarrett enters the screen, from nowhere it seems. He is in full flight and as the ball descends and without hesitation or loss of pace he takes the ball in his stride. He is unstoppable like the proverbial runaway train.

As if on a predestined track, arms pumping, knees like pistons, he takes a straight line. Nobody touches him. It was like the rest of his afternoon on the Arms Park that day, flawless.

Who would have thought that England in scoring 21 points should have lost.

What makes the try special is that prior to this one Vivian Jenkins had been the only full-back to score one for Wales.

Within a year or two, however, this last statistic would no longer retain any special meaning. In 1968 on a tour to

Colin McFadyean, a contemporary of the author at Loughborough, was the English player who kicked the ball to Jarrett at Cardiff in 1967. The rest is history.

(Press Association)

Argentina a new full-back was blooded who in his adventurous and courageous style would frequently find access to the try line, and if the line did not beckon for him, he would pave the way for others to benefit. With socks down to his ankles, in bravura style showing he meant business, and with hair flowing in his wake, JPR Williams entered into his domain, made the full-back position his own while at the same time redefining the role and illuminating the position's myriad possibilities. He had the derring-do to explore the potential rugby had to offer the full-back in the 1970s. He had an influential hand in many of the scintillating tries of that exceptional period.

Redefining the full-back position, J.P.R. Williams scored five tries against England in ten matches, this one at Twickenham in 1970.

(Press Association)

For that moment in the spring of 1967 we gloried in what the young Jarrett had so impeccably delivered. In hindsight we look back to wonder whether within this match and what we saw that day there lay a promise of an exciting time ahead not only for Wales but for rugby as a whole as it entered a new era. Was that day a prelude to the main narrative to come? And did not fearless Jarrett represent the epitome of the youthfulness, of the boldness, of the daring that lies at the essential heart of the game, indeed of the whole of sport?

KEITH JARRETT

1967

Rugby royalty. Keith Jarrett shakes hands with HRH, the Prince of Wales, before Wales play Ireland at Cardiff in 1969. He is introduced by captain Brian Price and flanked by the bearded John Taylor and Stuart Watkins.

(Press Association)

chards: 'a player

Maurice Richards: 'a player as scientist, not artist'.

(Colorsport)

Try 5

MAURICE RICHARDS v. NEW ZEALAND

Eden Park, Auckland
14 June, 1969

'Teachers open the door, but you must enter by yourself.'

Chinese proverb

I remember Maurice Richards as I first came across him. This was at a trial match in Ammanford in 1962. This was one among many a game we had to endure in order to be put under the microscopic gaze of the Welsh Secondary Schools selectors. It was a long path we had to trundle, many a mile to travel here and there, west and east to the numerous trials.

I had survived the Carmarthenshire one. I survived the Pembrokeshire one too but not at outside half where I had played all of my rugby at Queen Elizabeth Grammar School, Carmarthen. Brian Diment from Tenby played at Number 10 – and did so in a manner evocative of Richard Sharp – and I was ousted of my pretensions to the most lionised of positions. Diment later went on to play for Swansea against Australia in 1966 with Clive Rowlands as his scrum half.

The selectors with their new vision saw my international future at centre (as Clive Rowlands in New Zealand would later see fit to move me further out to the wing and closer to the touchline in 1969).

The Ammanford trial I remember not only because of Richards but also because of the warmth and affection I then felt because it was the first time my father came to see me play. He had stayed away on purpose hitherto.

The truth of the matter was that he had not encouraged me to play, avid supporter though he was of rugby and soccer, both of which he had played a great deal locally, and of Test match cricket, which he very much enjoyed watching on television. All in all, sport (and Aneurin Bevan) was his passion.

His lack of enthusiasm for my sporting involvement stemmed from two reasons. He himself had played but had on occasion suffered injuries. He had broken some bones in his time, he said. He did not want the same fate to befall me. This led on directly to the second reason. He did not want similar misfortunes to disrupt my school attendance. It was a mantra to him.

If Tony Blair could perorate about 'Education, Education, Education' my father had preceded him by some 50 years. It was a hard and fast rule in the house. He had been a collier who, one Friday afternoon after the end of the shift, had been told along with his brother, not to return on Monday. A medical inspection had showed too high a percentage of coal dust in his lungs and he was no longer deemed fit for work. He did work thereafter but an accident left him disabled for the rest of his life. Education would take me out of all this, he very strongly felt.

A child, however, will at times have his quietly obstinate way.

I loved the three sports my father much enjoyed. And since rugby at the grammar school was very much part of the curriculum (couldn't shirk part of my education?), and I had shown some interest (keen, I would say) and since the teachers insisted on picking me for their teams (I couldn't dissent and rebel against their authority), I felt I had no choice (had I?) but to give in (not exactly unwillingly) to their whims, and so eventually did my father. He was a regular presence at Stradey Park to watch and enthuse at Llanelli and was there, finally, in Ammanford to see his son play.

If his battle had been lost, it was never in any sense with regret.

'Education, education, education': the author at Cambridge University in 1968, 23 years old and still a student! (Press Association)

He followed every game after that, enthusiastically, although he hardly talked to me about it. I knew he could be voluble in his opinion of others and of rugby generally, but his presence was enough. I did not wish for more.

Maurice Richards's reputation had travelled ahead of him to Ammanford. He was a force to be reckoned with at centre. My experience in the centre on the other hand was minimal and I only had, after the selectors switched me to my new position, a few games at school to acclimatise.

Adults may fret and pine in sporting terms about a change of method or change of position. It concerned me only because I liked playing at outside half and a teacher had determined that, in his wisdom, that's where I might be most effective and could demonstrate best what gifts, if any, I had for the game. Being asked to move to the centre meant that I was still playing the game I loved and that another teacher had decided that Diment and I were both worthy of moving on to the next trial but that I was the one to make the shift. It was no great shakes.

Youngsters have no hang-ups about such things; no hopes are eternally dashed by such a change. A 17-year-old schoolboy is only a fleeting moment away from the footloose days in the gambolling playground where he played happy as the day is long. This was playtime. What matter where you played, so long as you played with the wind in your hair, the warm and satisfying perspiration on your face and healthily out of breath?

'Look away now!' The British Lions of 1968. Back, l-r: Bob Taylor, Keith Savage, Keith Jarrett, Norman Suddon, Roger Arneil, Jim Telfer, Willie John McBride, Peter Stagg, Peter Larter, Delme Thomas, John Pullin, Jeff Young, Maurice Richards, Bob Hiller (partially hidden), Tony Horton. Sitting, l-r: Gerald Davies, Barry Bresnihan, Sandy Hinshelwood, Syd Millar, John Taylor, John O'Shea, Gareth Edwards, Mike Gibson. On ground, l-r: Mick Doyle, Mike Coulman, Jock Turner, Barry John, Billy Raybould, Keri Jones, Roger Young, Gordon Connell.

(Colorsport)

And anyway, there has to be room for manoeuvre for the child to find his or her own way through such changes. Guidance not binding command is the wish. A gentle nudge is frequently better than the finger-wagging, fault-finding attempt at a fix.

This philosophy was born in me, especially, from an experience years later when ambition grew and great hopes hung, vividly but fancifully, in the air in the tower-block accommodation in Loughborough Colleges (enhanced to university status nowadays).

We had just played Swansea University in what was then the UAU Championship (the British Universities Cup today). Our much-fancied team had drawn, which meant a replay on the university grounds overlooking the lovely Swansea Bay. By my own estimation I had played badly. Dissatisfied and deeply dispirited, I plodded my weary way back to my room and, while the glimmering landscape faded at dusk, a hunched figure joined me along the path. It was John Robins, a man of major influence in my rugby career, as had been Bill Stanton at QEGS, Carmarthen, a mentor and guide. A sportsman, like others, needs the kindness of good people.

Robins sympathised. All he said, shoulders hunched and beneath a pair of shaggy eyebrows, was 'Recognise and understand how you feel at this moment. You don't want to feel like this again.' He was a man of few words, carefully chosen. It was a significant and pivotal moment for me. I carried those two sentences, simple but with such a profound meaning, with me for all time. As if looking over my shoulder, I can see vividly, slipping back, the exact place now, changeless and irremovable, and hear the words. I can almost smell what little I ate that evening.

As with the best of teachers, they guide, encourage in such a way that inspires the pupil to think that he or she has found the answer to the conundrum, to draw their own conclusions. Not for the teacher to give the answer immediately, but through hints and gestures urging the pupil to experience his or her own Eureka moment and sense of triumph.

All this is a long way off from Maurice Richards, whose reputation had arrived ahead of him. He had at 18 already played for Cardiff. Clearly he was to be a formidable opponent, someone to be reckoned with.

He was a brilliant player. He was tall and sinewy, raw-boned and long of leg, one whose elongated strides lent him a lancing quickness.

'He had a lean and hungry look about him…' Maurice Richards dribbles past Ireland's Tom Kiernan at Cardiff in 1969.

(Colorsport/Colin Elsey)

'Aggressive and incisive', Maurice Richards breaks this French tackle at Cardiff in 1968.   (Press Association)

Delme Thomas, with bulging left biceps, tries to win the ball for Wales against England in 1969. His line-out take would later lead to Richards's fourth and final try.

(Press Association)

There was nothing soft in him. He was sharp-angled, without a wasted ounce on his frame. He had a lean and hungry look about him. Such men, I had read, were dangerous.

He was aggressive and incisive; his skills were acute and finely distilled to the essential needs of the moment. He had extravagant gifts but never used them prodigally. He was a player as scientist not artist. Everything seemed to be calculated, computed geometrically. He scored four tries against England in 1969, which matched the international try-scoring record in one match.

His final try at the Arms Park that day shows the essence of Richards's play. The ball is moved from Delme Thomas's win at the line-out to Edwards to John. In response to centre Jarrett's pass Richards straightens the line to come between John Spencer and David Duckham in midfield. With sheer pace he avoids others on the way and reaches the line with Duckham, having recovered, hanging on to his shoulders.

His mind was as tough as his body. He was a tenacious competitor. In my way of undeveloped thinking, he was utterly unsentimental and case-hardened, I sensed, rightly or wrongly, by the densely populated Rhondda which was so unlike my softer, rural background.

After Ammanford we both went on to play for the Welsh Secondary Schools in 1963 at centre.

The try I choose is not one of his schoolboy scorchers or one of his Arms Park quartet. However it was not recorded for posterity. After the Triple Crown win in 1969, Wales travelled for the first time to New Zealand. Having lost the first Test in Christchurch 19–0, the second Test was in Auckland. Wales played well that day. At 3–3 after 20 minutes Richards was given the ball just outside the All Black 22-metre line. With a number of players converging on him, including the outstanding full-back Fergie McCormick, Richards feinted to run inside, checked his speed, halted the defence, and then, with acceleration and with with an outrageous outside swerve, at least four defenders were left dumbfounded at the sheer elan and effrontery of the devastating run. That McCormick, whose red-blooded tackling had an aura of invincibility, should have had the

Seizing the game by the throat, David Duckham takes on Australia's Paddy Batch at Twickenham in 1976. The Englishman had less of a hold on Maurice Richards at Cardiff in 1969. (Colorsport)

misfortune to have been laid waste by Richards left New Zealand dumb.

The game was a good competition at this stage until the New Zealand referee took a hand in matters and made some suspicious decisions which lacked, in his interpretation of the laws, shall we say, finesse. Wales lost 33–12.

Maurice Richards's try was a worthy memory in the same way as Jonathan Davies's 60-metre run for a try under the posts against the same opposition would be at the same venue 19 years later. Again in what was another heavy loss (54–9), it remains the solitary consolation.

1969

MAURICE RICHARDS

'No one plays like Barry John anymore.'
(Colorsport/Colin Elsey)

BARRY JOHN
v. ENGLAND

National Stadium, Cardiff
12 April, 1969

'In gallant trim the gilded vessel goes,
Youth on the prow, and Pleasure at the helm.'

'Oxford', Thomas Gray

'Some players play with the wind, others create it,' Carwyn James
once wrote in his unmissable, unmistakably allusive and lucid articles
in *The Guardian*. His Friday pieces became essential reading, just
as compelling in their own way as his soft-hued reflections in the
television studio of BBC Wales's Sunday rugby programme. Nowadays
TV executives are suspicious of talking heads; back then Carwyn
simply talked to the camera, often without visual representation to
illustrate what he had to say, and his words transfixed us with clever
and insightful views on any rugby topic that took his fancy.

Among those who create the wind's flow belonged Barry John.
He was unique, an original in his graceful and unlaboured style of
play. 'We shall not see his like again' is so overused as a valedictory
compliment that it has become a cliché. However it is safe to say that

A refined authority: Carwyn James, coach of the 1971 British Lions. (Press Association)

'There's daggers in men's smiles'. Barry John's nonchalance belied a sharp, competitive edge.

(Colorsport/Colin Elsey)

it is apt in Barry John's case. The try against England in 1969, when the Arms Park had been reduced to building-site rubble as the new stadium was being built and re-shaped, identifies his art. If his try that day was a noble testament to his skills, the backdrop was rather shabby, not at all the regal theatre his 'Kingship' deserved.

That James should write for *The Guardian* accorded fittingly with the tradition of what was originally the *Manchester Guardian* and which had spawned Neville Cardus as the doyen of cricket reporters and essayists. Mixing prose and poetry, they thrived on the colour of saying, admitting their unswerving passion for what happened or was about to happen on the greensward. Whereas Cardus, drawing from his love of music, saw in cricket the harmony between a player's style of play at the crease and his character and manner, James loved and understood the evolving drama of rugby in the way he enjoyed the gradual unfolding of a plot from the playhouse gallery.

Both writers loved the performance and the sense of theatre and were masterly in providing a vivid picture of their practical and imaginative vision of their sport. There was, then, in both men a hinterland of interest beyond cricket's boundary and rugby's touchline respectively, which allowed them to acquire, through their freshness, tone and grace, a different level of refined authority which spoke to a delighted and discerning readership.

Whither Barry John? Whither the wind in today's rugby climate? Such questions are asked because of the changing nature of rugby. Where would he be now in a game inhabited by behemoths, players measured daily in vitamin-intake and carbohydrates, of unlimited hours in the gym and GPS control? The rugby world has moved on and, for better and for worse, changed irrevocably.

Thankfully, there is room still for the 'special one', the one touched by genius, and since this is Wales, let us talk of Shane Williams and Leigh Halfpenny. There are others elsewhere. They create a wave and a current, and though they are but miniatures in comparison to the giants that surround them, the game is the better for seeing that they can, after all, rise above the predilection for bulk. They can shift swiftly and adroitly to avoid the titan's lengthening shadows. Agile and nimble, quick of mind and deed, they can still rule the rugby world, and the joy they bring increases our admiration and gratitude.

Rugby union in the 21st Century has taken on another character. The new shape of the professional player has partly determined that

Like Barry John, Shane Williams was 'touched by genius'. Here he sidesteps French prop Jean-Baptiste Poux in the Rugby World Cup semi-final in 2011.

(Colorsport/Andrew Cowie)

this should be so. The unlimited time afforded the full-time player to prepare physically and mentally has made a huge contribution. Coaches with a strong background in rugby league have exerted an influence on the shape the game has recently and radically adopted. Going hand in hand with this freedom for the players and their coaches is the intensive analysis that accompanies the coaching. Television has played its part, too, in that with so much comprehensive coverage and with so many cameras in attendance at every televised game, there is footage galore to look at; every tackle to replay and inspect; every twist of the elbow, every feint to scrutinise and reduce to frame-by-frame analysis. There is a head coach, a backs coach, defence coach, a kicking coach, and so the list adjusts itself according to the

Ball in two hands, Barry John glides past Irish defenders at Cardiff in 1969. In moustachioed support is the author.

(Colorsport/Colin Elsey)

tactical minutiae and the individual strengths and weaknesses that require attention at any given time.

This change is clearly manifest when we see recorded television footage of Barry John play. The 'then' and 'now', and the vast chasm of difference in between, is revealed. It brooks no argument. Rugby is different.

No one plays like Barry John anymore; they are unable to do so or, the suspicion is that they are not allowed to because of the changes in patterns of play; or by instruction, since coaches by and large are very wary or simply cannot understand the instinctive genius of players such as John. Frankly, it defies analysis.

He had poise and balance and played on impulse. He had the allure of a ladies' man, slim and attractive, a touch of feminine delicacy in his every movement which would be so out of place among the stubbled cheeks and towering proportions of today's Brobdingnagians.

He was a blatantly romantic figure, a delicate grace, languorous and elusive, with a carefree charm both on and off the field. He was never unknowing of how good he was. He nonetheless had an attractive line in self-deprecation. Congratulated on a try-saving push on Dauga the French number 8 at Stade Colombes in Wales's Grand Slam victory in 1971 and having broken his nose in the effort, he responded 'Thank you for the kind words… but what I want to know is… who pushed me?!'

If there were titans in his day, he dismissed them with a mischievous wink – as was truly his wont – as he glided beyond their threatening arms. No snarling back-row forward, or anyone else for that matter, could enslave him such was his faith that he could do whatever he chose in the instant to do. The pitch was his domain which he ruled not with an iron fist but with a wily will. He controlled a game much as a conductor might his orchestra, pointing here and there, directing a pass one moment and then, the next, a sly kick, high or low, to the confusion of his opponents.

'The pitch was his domain': Barry John scores against England in 1970. The Twickenham crowd in the background are less than ecstatic.

(Press Association)

Another 'special one'. Ball in two hands, Lions full-back Leigh Halfpenny leaves Australia's Joe Tomane in his wake during the third Test at Sydney in July 2013.

(Press Association)

Nonchalantly, he once pronounced in his very early days at Cardiff Arms Park, after he had moved from Llanelli, that when he saw a pretty girl in the crowd on the 22-metre line the thought might occur to him that this vision of delight might determine his choice of where he should place the next kick. He was committed to a stylishly relaxed approach to life and to sport. The opposition would bend to his seductive will while those in his company would be lured by his carefree charm.

His hand-eye co-ordination was exemplary, allied to an instinctive feel and nous for playing football and rugby. He nurtured a consistent individualism but was not as egotistical as to ignore the value of what it is to play in a team. He might he have appeared aloof but he was a team player and a boon companion.

He left the field of play with his kit hardly needing to be laundered and did so with a smile and an insouciant shrug. But his easy-going

Barry John about to press the trigger against England at Cardiff in 1972. (Press Association)

appeal should not disguise the sharp determination of the competitors' sliver of ice beneath the casual surface. He had his winning ways on and off the field.

He was a confidence trickster, readjusting his shape and positions so as to make the other side look heavy-footed and clumsy, their upper bodies having been persuaded to go one way while the lower half would be speeding in the opposite direction, leaving their faces looking bewildered, much like the gravity-defying characters in the 'Road Runner' cartoons.

The epitome of his style was the try he scored against England in 1969 at the Arms Park. The movement began when Keith Jarrett's awkward pass falls behind John Dawes. Barry picks it up and wends his way silkily to the try line, leaving four defenders, arms outstretched, to feel the warmth of the airflow left in his wake.

Dave Rollitt, England's no. 8 finally gets to him but too late. John has touched down for a try.

This is a favourite try not only because of the contrast between what the game was in 1971 (where I belonged and about which I am inevitably sentimental) and what it has become in the 21st century, but because Barry's try against England represents the glory of the game as it once was. There were long uneventful periods and moments of leaden inactivity. But they did not seem like that at the time. The game was the way it was, with nothing to compare it with, unlike today.

Similarly against Scotland in 1971 where he glides his way for a try. It was a Scot, the great sports writer Norman Mair, who observed that year: 'It is with considerable relief to witness Barry John enter a room by the doorway rather than materialise through the wall.' Bill McLaren thought him 'a phantom'.

Nowadays the objective is to knock down the wall and charge forcefully through.

John's artistic style was not modest but it was young at heart and... fun.

He was of his time. Such movement, frictionless and suave; such players do not exist nowadays.

John Dawes leads Wales out against Ireland at Cardiff in 1971. (Press Association)

BARRY JOHN

Graham Price, 'an outstanding tight-head prop'.

(Colorsport)

Graham Price
v. France

Parc des Princes, Paris
18 January, 1975

'We are the sons of flint and pitch.'

'I See the Boys of Summer', Dylan Thomas

These pages are full of wonderful tries. There are others of exceptional quality which have missed the cut, to use a golfer's phrase. They could well have been included. To bring the guillotine down after making the choice is obviously difficult. Others in my position would have chosen otherwise.

One thing is certain. Tries scored by a forward would be rare. These pages are dominated by tries scored by the backs. The piano players, as the French would have it, outnumber the piano shifters. Or to put it another way, as is frequently said, if it is the forwards who invariably determine who the victor should be, it is the back division who determine by how much. It is a convenient summary.

As with every cliché there is an element of truth which never quite manages to tell the whole truth. We can all find examples which

International try scorers all! The Pontpool front row, from left to right, Graham Price, Bobby Windsor and 'Charlie' Faulkner, in action for the Lions in New Zealand in 1977.

(Colorsport)

tell a different story. Within these pages, for example, you will find a Ieuan Evans try against England in 1993 where Wales's forwards were outclassed, so that by chance, the slimmest of opportunities was grabbed by Wales's winger to run some 70 metres to score a winning try. It was against the run of play in much the same way as was Scott Gibbs's try at Wembley against England in 1999. Rugby is a better game for enabling the maverick or the rogue moment. The tale of the unexpected is what ultimately adds piquancy to the joy of sporting competition.

From my own personal experience is a quarter-final cup match between Pontypool and Cardiff in 1977: Pontypool dominated the possession and controlled every facet of the forward contest, but it was Cardiff who won the match and marched on to the semi-final.

There have been some great tries scored by forwards, going back to Cliff Davies against England in 1950, and in 1957 to Bryn Meredith against France, after a movement initiated by Lloyd Williams in the Welsh 22, continued by Gordon Wells and finished by the (then) London Welsh hooker. You also have Bobby Windsor against

Australia in 1973, 'Charlie' Faulkner against Ireland in 1975 and Bob Norster against Ireland in 1987.

There are the back-row forwards, of course, who must include the hugely skilful John Taylor with his tries in 1969, 1971 and 1972, each one showing how the skills he had acquired once as a centre transferred to his benefit as a flanker. He was an exceptional player as an out-and-out open-side wing forward. He had antennae which were sensitively in tune, knowing where next most usefully to be. He was partnered by Dai Morris, who had a similar awareness, as summed up by his nickname 'Shadow'. He was always next to the important player, always arriving spot on time.

Then there was the father-and-son combination who scored not too dissimilar tries in Cardiff: father Derek Quinnell fending off three would-be Scottish tacklers along the touchline towards the River Taff end of the ground in 1978, and son Scott on the same flank

Scott Quinnell outstrips France's Philippe Saint-Andre (no. 11) and Abdelatif Benazzi on his way to the line at Cardiff in 1994, as Gareth Llewellyn offers long-distance support.

(Colorsport/Andrew Cowie)

A graduate of the Pontypool Ballet School, Graham Price is outleapt by Lions colleague Maurice Colclough against the All Blacks in 1983.

(Colorsport)

A frank exchange of views: Geoff Wheel and England's Bill Beaumont thrash out some issues at Twickenham in 1980. It was Wheel's relieving kick which led to Graham Price's finest hour in Paris in 1975.

(Colorsport/Colin Elsey)

but running towards the Westgate end against France in 1994. These were great tries, showing determination, speed, composure and of knowing where the try line was and how best in the most direct way to get there. Either Quinnell try could enter the pantheon. What a dynasty of rugby people they are: Derek's wife and Scott's mother is Madora, the sister of Barry John, with another son, Craig, also playing for Wales and scoring a try against France in 1999.

But it is to Graham Price, of Pontypool, Wales and Lions I must turn. He scored what can only be thought of as a spectacular try on his debut match for Wales in 1975. Perhaps 'sensational' would be more appropriate, except that this word has lost some of its currency and value. It is now more redolent of the red-carpeted ostentation of tinsel-town premieres and their flash-photography flashiness. Price was not of this kind.

It might also describe the more lurid tales of shocking goings-on, usually involving someone very rich or aristocratic or in government caught *in flagrante*, or at least disappearing somewhere abroad never to be seen again.

This last image might resonate in Pontypool, especially with those humorists who might be aware of the reputation the rugby club had and the jibes they had to confront because of the limited style of their rugby tactics. This was based on a furious forward commitment which was at the time awesome in its power and selfless dedication. It was dour and combative and superbly efficient in gaining and keeping possession. It was so strenuously aggressive that it was often mistaken for violent intent. This was unjust. The commanding figure, father-figure of many of the players, who ruled Pontypool Park for almost 20 years as coach, was the inimitable Ray Prosser.

They were quite fond of telling stories against themselves. If the ball reached the Pontypool outside half, it was generally conceded that a passing movement had taken place. To be sure, in this severe, loyal and disciplined environment, to play on the wing was to be consigned to solitary confinement. It was a no-man's land, a bourn from which no traveller returns.

This gave rise to the quip about Lord Lucan, who one evening in the 1974 fled into the night never to be seen again. Except, he had been seen, it was claimed: 'He's playing on the wing for Pontypool'.

Sensational? Graham Price's try certainly was worthy of the word. It was sensational. It was exciting and needed a flourish of trumpets.

To my way of thinking, the word describes a performance of striking excellence engraved in the memory. The try, gradually evolving, improbable and utterly unprepared for, was supremely tantalising – will he? won't he? – and, to justify the 'sensation', was eminently and grandly theatrical.

The plot was laid deep in Wales's own territory. To begin with, Wales simply looked to have escaped from the mounting momentum of French attack. Wales, in the form of Geoff Wheel, hacked out of defence.

It was greeted with simple relief; imprisoned and shackled, as they had been, there had been no room for Wales to manoeuvre. Wales could not get their hands on the ball so that when it finally went loose, they were glad to have got out of jail. There was no other expectation, no more than simply letting the time run out so that Wales, already ahead, would gain an unexpected and remarkable win in Paris.

If Wales had overcome France four years earlier at Stade Colombes to win the Grand Slam, they had to go back to 1957 for the previous success in Paris. Crossing the Channel was a daunting task. The language was different, the all-pervading smell of the Gitanes cigarettes was prominent and you could not escape the taste of garlic in all the food. There was a tangible difference.

These grew in the mind in such a way as to make them seem to be insurmountable obstacles, as if any of these cultural and social differences should play a part in a game of rugby. This self-made psychological intimidation was embedded long before any departure from Rhoose Airport (as it then was) and was made worse by the constant reference to how good the French were with the warmth of the Spring sunshine on their backs. Playing France in those days meant the fixture fell in April. Such fears have evaporated today as the current crop of players is more familiar with crossing boundaries and of travelling far afield. They are international players in every sense.

Mervyn Davies, captain of Wales on Graham Price's international debut in Paris. Also making his debut that day was Ray Gravell, seen here taking the pitch with Davies for the Barbarians against Australia in 1976.

(Colorsport/Colin Elsey)

Furthermore, the 1975 team was thoroughly inexperienced and included six new caps. The Pontypool front row of Tony 'Charlie' Faulkner, Bobby Windsor and Price appeared together for the first time. Wales had a new coach in John Dawes and a new captain in Mervyn Davies.

Graham Price's try was a unique piece of international rugby action which has never been equalled. In its style, context, manner and scorer, it was an extraordinary try. It was an 80-metre run, completed by a 23-year-old debutant prop forward who had scrummaged in a tough tussle against a mighty French pack, and scored in the game's final few minutes.

Graham Price was an outstanding tight-head prop who had accomplished much at a very tender age. Educated at West Monmouthshire Grammar School, he had not only played for the Welsh Secondary Schools in 1970 but had also played for Pontypool whilst still a schoolboy. The following year he appeared for the Monmouthshire under 25 XV against the Canadians, all this before he was 20 years of age.

He proved himself one of the world's best scrummagers, but he was more than a superb player in the tight matters of the game. He had a good all-round ability as a rugby player. He was fast, too, as illustrated by the great try at Parc des Princes.

That he, the cornerstone of the scrum at tight-head, should have scored the try was a remarkable feat. He had had his work cut out all afternoon to withstand the force of a heavyweight scrum. It was hard slog in difficult conditions. The soft surface made it unsteady underfoot.

As Wales's thin red line resisted the relentless French siege, they suddenly enjoyed a stroke of good luck. France lost direction and cohesion. Confusion as to where to go next against Wales's firm defence saw Jean Pierre Lux turn back towards his forwards. He lost his grip on the ball.

As it fell to the ground, Geoff Wheel hacked it upfield, as far as the halfway line. Racing ahead of everyone and arriving at the ball first, Price gave the ball another hefty boot.

The field was wide open, the try line beckoned from afar. The French defence, split and in disarray, was nonetheless closing in. But though the remnants of the France three-quarter line surged desperately back, Price, a prop, looked to have the stamina and

A Price on the floor is worth two for the Bush. New Zealand prop Billy Bush tries to reason with Graham Price during the second Lions Test in 1977. All Black elder statesmen Ian Kirkpatrick and Sid Going look on in solemn admiration.

(Colorsport)

the swifter legs despite the afternoon's energy-sapping efforts. J.J. Williams was also on hand to give a further nudge away from the feet of a Frenchman. With the ball just dropping short of the try line, Price had the composure and the steady hands to swoop for a famous try.

At which point Nigel Starmer-Smith, the commentator, almost breathless himself, found the words which echoed what most of us thought after witnessing the extraordinary efforts : 'They'll never believe it in Pontypool,' he enthused. They did.

At Pontypool, props were expected to be in the forefront and grab the headlines. They were the stars. What they would not credit at the beautiful Pontypool Park was when a winger was allowed to score such a try from such a distance. Now that was hard to believe.

1975

GRAHAM PRICE

Yet another Price try! Graham Price dips and swivels his way to the line against Ireland in 1977. Bobby Windsor in support finds it amusing.

(Colorsport)

Phil Bennett: scorer, some say, of the greatest Welsh try ever...

(Press Association)

Try 8

PHIL BENNETT
v. SCOTLAND

Murrayfield, Edinburgh
19 March, 1977

'Where an equal poise of hope and fear
Does arbitrate th' event, my nature is
That inclined to hope rather than fear.'

'Comus', John Milton

Choosing a try in which I had been personally involved was always going to create its own problems!

To Clive Rowlands and Robert Jones, it is the best Welsh try ever. In fact, as co-presenters of their *101 Great Welsh Tries* DVD, they even suggested it might be the greatest in all international rugby. Who am I, therefore, to disagree with two such great former players, both of whom remain keen observers of the rugby scene?

In any case, though I dare say so myself, I also feel that it is undeniably a great try.

At Murrayfield in 1977 it was Phil Bennett who was finally the one to place the ball over the line with a firm hand before resting his chin on the ball as well. Under the crossbar he cast his eyes back as if wistfully pondering on the screwed passage of adventurous play and replaying the many clever judgements that had prompted Bill McLaren to conclude 'Surely, the try of the season'. The chin on the ball was a kind of full stop, as if to say 'that should put an end to it'.

If poetry and song have helped provide the Welsh man and woman with a vision of what it is to be Welsh, it is because uplifting romance and mystical melancholy often inspire both, and such instinctive feelings also run through and haunt our affections for rugby. It is a somewhat up-and-down affair. Underlying the drama is a strong seam of humour and of mischief, and of what Richard Burton once called 'the massive lies and stupendous exaggerations'.

Wizard or not, with the ball or not, Lions captain Phil Bennett is not about to escape the clutches of the All Blacks at Auckland in 1977, especially since one of his tacklers is Ian Kirkpatrick (no. 7). Looking on in red, from left to right, are Douglas Morgan, Tony Neary and a prostrate Willie Duggan. (Colorsport)

For instance, you need only mention the day Llanelli beat the All Blacks: if you believe all those who claim to have been there then the whole population of Wales must have acquired a ticket to be in Stradey Park on that overcast day of overflowing delight in 1972. Phil Bennett was there to steer a course to a mammoth victory.

It is, of course, the longing and the unending quest for moments of inspiring reverie that really matters. The thud and blunder, the pushing and shoving, is worth the patience only if, even now and again, we can abandon ourselves to the fleeting and exhilarating joy of the grand and clever, uninterrupted move. Within which there lies daring and, let us say, mischief which, in turn, lends itself to a sense of fun.

Phil's try explores these characteristics in full. But there are also moments when the whole edifice might have fallen apart, when you are forced to hold your breath as the pass might not have been well-aimed or not held or gone astray. Luck, as ever, plays its part as well as the players' natural gifts to allow the move, miraculously, to survive and achieve greatness.

It is so with the greatest of tries, the one scored by the Barbarians in 1973 against New Zealand in what was still then Cardiff Arms Park. Once more we find Bennett demonstrating his wizardry and thrice he gets away from the clutches of the All Blacks. His long looped pass finds JPR Williams, who almost gets throttled but manages – just – to get the ball away to John Pullin. A little later, you have to hold your breath: Derek Quinnell has to pick up the ball from his toes at top speed. There the move could have faltered and petered out. But, thankfully, it did not and Gareth Edwards scores in the corner.

And so it was in a 1977.

For a long period before Phil scored, Wales – we – had been on our heels as wave upon wave of navy blue jerseys launched attack upon attack. We were beleaguered, living a life at siege, surviving by our fingertips. We did not, it seems, touch the ball for a lifetime; moving left and right we were forced to follow Scotland's whims and fancies – chasing shadows, it seems. With the likes of Andy Irvine and Jim Renwick, fast and with flair and masters of attack, Scotland were in rampant mood

But they became frustrated: our defence stayed true and we kept them at bay, so in desperation they kicked ahead in an attempt to

break the deadlock. This proved to be a wrong call. They gave away the ball which hitherto we had failed to win by our own ability. We had possession at last. It was a deadly misjudgement by Scotland but one in the circumstances understandable.

The chip over the top was not too far ahead, just enough for JPR to be the first to retrieve it for Wales, and he did so on his knees. He flipped it to Steve Fenwick, a wonderfully calm and controlled centre. Living on the game's edge, the chance needed to be grasped.

Fenwick slipped to me. This took McLaren by surprise in the commentary box. 'What's Davies doing there?' he queried. I was there to fill in the gaps left by Scotland's constant pressure. We had to arrange and re-arrange the defence according to Scotland's relentless attacks, varying the lines and direction of their running. I couldn't stay purposeless and disengaged far out on the wing.

A kick by me would not solve our increasing dilemmas. It would simply return the ball to our opponents. We might not see it again for quite a while. It was time to run.

A couple of sidesteps inwards and to the left off my right foot proved a starting point. One art of the sidestep is to change such a one-dimensional inward pattern, one whose repetitive rhythm is so compelling that it does not need thinking about. As such, it can often lead ultimately to the arms of the opponent who has anticipated your next move. However, changing this pattern is not easy, and is especially difficult to accomplish at speed.

My initial sidesteps had been taking me back to where the defence was thickest. A change was needed. So to the right I went, my hand off giving me added momentum, and out towards support in the shape of David Burcher. He delayed momentarily and wisely – this is the moment where it could have broken down – to give an overhead pass which had

'Fast and with flair and masters of attack', Jim Renwick (above) and Andy Irvine (below) were part of a Scottish team that were in rampant mood before Phil Bennett's spectacular try at Murrayfield in 1977.
(Colorsport)

Leaders of men. Phil Bennett and the author lead out, respectively, the British Lions and the Barbarians at Twickenham in 1977. Behind them are two who, tragically, are no longer with us: Gordon Brown (left) and Ray Gravell (middle).

(Colorsport/Colin Elsey)

'Bennett... knowing who's there, without a glance or a check, sidesteps...' Phil Bennett off on another of his jinking runs, this time against Japan at Cardiff in 1974. From left to right, the Welsh players looking on are Clive Shell, Roy Bergiers, Mervyn Davies, J.J. Williams and John Taylor who is obscured by Derek Quinnell.

(Colorsport)

'hopeful' written all over it. (There are players in between, such passes lacks accuracy and can be disrupted.) It works. Steve Fenwick could have been smothered but the centre, beautifully and instinctively, shifts the ball inside in one move, to Bennett and he, knowing who's there, without a glance or check, sidesteps inside the last flailing defender.

Each player had played his part, holding his nerve, knowing what was possible and executing what was needed. It was wonderful to have had a part in it.

Over the years I have been asked to choose my favourite try of those I have scored myself. I can't truly answer the question because such decisions may be determined by any such try's degree of difficulty, or its manner or its match context and so on. After all, someone appearing on *Desert Island Discs* on Radio 4 may presumably make one choice of eight records this week before making an entirely different choice the following week.

So it is with tries.

The wing is the finisher usually. In this case I have to admit that the degree of difficulty mattered for me. Was there anything left for me to accomplish or was it a matter of taking the ball over the line? Taking the ball over the line was part of a team effort and it gave enormous satisfaction, of course. It is what we were there to do. It could also be interpreted as simply a statistic in the ledger.

As I say, I enjoyed the challenge. If there is vanity in this then so be it. Dare I say, as in every performer, there is always the desire to prove what you can do, to show off, if you like, to flaunt whatever talent you may think you have. This spurs you on. There is a selfish gene in every performer so long as it works ultimately for the good of the team.

Bennett scores the first of two tries against France, as he leads Wales to Grand Slam triumph at Cardiff in 1978. (Press Association)

So, being part of that try in Scotland in that way is the sweetest of memories for me. That gave me more satisfaction than many a try I scored. I wanted to play what I considered to be a distinctive part. As a former outside half and centre, I relished the need to be involved. As a wing, I did not wish simply to be the man at the end of the line, a runner-in of tries. I wanted to create something different, and not loiter only with intent, waiting for something to happen. It might take a long time, especially in those days when statistics indicate that the ball was only in play for some 23 minutes of the game, whereas nowadays it is 40 minutes. Action was required.

This may go some way to answer the great Bill McLaren's question: 'What's Davies doing there?'

My contribution only carried on what JPR and Fenwick had started and what Burcher, Fenwick (again) and Bennett finished. In other words it was a team effort with daring players willing to take a chance and with a sense of adventure in their hearts.

1977

PHILL BENNETT

Bennett the provider this time, setting up Ray Gravell against England at Twickenham in 1976.

(Press Association)

Adrian Hadley, eyeing the line at Twickenham again.

(Press Association)

ADRIAN HADLEY
v. ENGLAND

Twickenham, London
6 February, 1988

'Fe ddaeth yr atgof eto'n glir
Megis o'r môr ar lam
– Y dydd y cyrchais dros y lein
Â'r bêl yn Twickenham...'

(The mem'ry leapt so clearly back,
As from the sea, once more
– The day I ventured o'er the line
At Twickenham to score...)

'Y Dyrfa', Cynan.

In choosing the great tries, the instinctive response, by and large, is to recollect the triumph of a single player, the touch of the master's hand, the eye-catching exploit which transports us to the realms of chivalric derring-do. It is not necessarily the right way to choose.

In this personal collection it is the overcoming of impossible odds, the remaining in possession of wits and the sure-footed craft of the single player romping home which has prevailed. Invariably, even when there is dash of good fortune, a slice of luck, it is so easy to think only of the special one, of the lone name attached to the magical score, and momentarily to pass by other players who have set the platform to make the whole thing possible in the first place.

What then of the team try? What of the panoramic scope, of the contortions and curves, the swing and sinuous span of the collective

*'David... Tom David... The halfway line.'
The Llanelli and Wales wing forward,
though tackled by Peter Whiting, keeps the
hopes of a great Barbarians try alive, whilst
Bob Burgess and Sandy Carmichael (with
headband) look on.* (Press Association)

effort: the many hands and brave efforts, the gathering momentum and
the growing sense of hope, finally reaching breathlessly, disbelievingly,
the try line?

'What a score!' rejoices Cliff Morgan, as Gareth Edwards flies
sublimely through the air for the most paraded try of all time, *that*
1973 Barbarians score against the All Blacks at the Arms Park in
Cardiff. Here is the late Cliff Morgan's enduring narrative:

'Williams again... Everyone with him... Sid Going... Very little
support... Good tackle by Slattery... of Ireland... Almost to the
halfway line... Kirkpatrick to Williams... Oooh, this is great stuff!
Brilliant (*Bennett's first sidestep*)... Oooh (*second sidestep*)...That's
brilliant (*third sidestep*)... John Williams...Pullin... John Dawes...
Oooh.... Great dummy... David... Tom David.... The halfway
line.... Oooh... Brilliant... by Quinnell. This is Gareth Edwards...
A dramatic start! What a score... Oooooooh... That fellow
Edwards!'

In 1993 I decided to quote this piece of commentary in a piece I was writing for *The Times* about the Barbarians and on the twentieth anniversary of the great game.

This was to illustrate Cliff Morgan's economy with words: how they must fit the picture and how the best commentators understand that what they say is subordinate, a guide, to what the viewers actually see. Economy is the key, impartiality too. To declare his enthusiasm as Cliff does is not the same as taking sides.

He is as elated and animated with what the All Blacks are attempting to do – 'Oh, this is great stuff', as Sid Going and Bryan Williams begin their running before the fateful high kick deep into Barbarians territory – as much as he is with what the Barbarians are beginning to do. 'Brilliant…' he thrills, as Bennett starts the adventurous and tantalising route, under his own posts in the shadow of the North Stand at the Westgate end of the Arms Park, to the final deified revelation underneath the South Stand at the Taff end.

These words are now as familiar and – excepting Kenneth Wolstenholme's 'They think it's all over… It is now', from the 1966 football World Cup final at Wembley – the most repeated television sporting commentary of these islands.

This is still the ultimate, the most beloved of tries, the best of rugby football, because now and then we need to look beyond the clutter and the roughhouse nature of the game and spy, even if it is through rose-tinted glasses, the game's grace and beauty. This is what we witnessed from the Barbarians that January day. It remains rugby's most cherished moment.

Wales managed on occasions to come close to matching such excitement.

A firm favourite is the 1973 try against Ireland by London Welsh winger Jim Shanklin, father of Tom. Once more, and in the same season, it is Phil Bennett who works his wonder with a brand of wizardry not dissimilar to the magic he wove against the All Blacks a few weeks earlier.

Once again within his own 22-metre line, he recovers a long kick from Ireland. Although he has JPR in support, Phil decides to pursue his own independent course. One sidestep, a second sidestep and he casts another of his enchantments. It is potentially treacherous, certainly a wishful gamble of high stakes. And what is rugby without such gambles? It ends in a spellbinding finale at the Westgate end of the stadium.

Welsh centre Jim Shanklin, who was at the end of a 'firm favourite' of a try, against Ireland in 1973. (Press Association)

The third best team in the world... Adrian Hadley's try is about to be followed by Paul Thorburn's touchline conversion to give Wales a dramatic 22–21 victory over Australia in the third-place play-off in Rotorua at the 1987 Rugby World Cup, as Michael Lynagh arrives too late.

(Colorsport/Colin Elsey)

Glyn Shaw, in his own half, plucks from the air Phil's high pass. The prop forward 'really can run,' observes McLaren. And so he goes on to Ireland's 10-metre line. John Taylor moves it on and is tackled by Mike Gibson. Mervyn Davies forages for the ball ten yards out from the Irish line. Dai Morris, the 'Shadow' as ever, hands on to Edwards on the narrow side underneath the old North Stand, going past three would-be tackles and running dangerously close to the touchline. His one-handed pass inside gives Shanklin the try.

We can go back to 1957 and Bryn Meredith's try against France for such long-range tries of adventurousness, started by Lloyd Williams and Gordon Wells in their own 25-yard line. This was at a time when it was France's reputation to score such flamboyant tries, not Wales. The try by Meredith, one of the world's great hookers, is a beautiful piece of Welsh extravagance at a time when matches were won narrowly on penalties.

Finally, my choice of best team try will settle on Adrian Hadley's try against England at Twickenham in 1988. But which one? He scored two that day. There is little that separates them in terms of enterprise and daring. It is a difficult choice. It is the execution that becomes the deciding factor.

There are two basic errors of passing in the first try when the move might have come to a halt. It does not prove to be a smooth, uninterrupted passage of play. Late in the movement near England's 22-metre line the ball goes loose and Richie Collins, for the second time in the move, picks up and passes to Robert Norster, who had won the ball in the line-out in his own half in the first instance to start the long play. Norster checks one pass and changes his mind, giving instead an overhead pass which seemed to be bound for Hadley but which goes to ground. Bowen picks up, before Hadley receives the ball to avoid the covering Cusworth, the English outside half, for the try.

It is the other one that gets the vote. There is greater clarity and precision.

There were four Welshmen playing that day who were recognised as outside halves and they are all involved in the score, two of them twice. They were all immensely talented players, each with vision and the desire to run instinctively. They were not manufactured.

It all begins with Tony Clement at full-back. It is he, courageously, who initiates the movement, taking a high kick from Les Cusworth near his own 22. Under pressure he keeps his head and avoids two English players, Rory Underwood and Will Carling. Bleddyn Bowen is in support, is held, and his pass runs loose. Wade Dooley intercepts and attempts to recover but loses control. Jonathan Davies picks up the momentum and hands to Mark Ring.

Each of the players so far is an outside half for his club but now occupying other positions for Wales. Ring of Cardiff to Clement of Swansea, Clement to Hadley, the Cardiff winger, and so back to Ring who, once more, finds Hadley in support with the winger having run around infield to receive Ring's return pass. The winger veers outside to avoid England's covering defence.

It is a marvellous try with each player in unhurried control of his movement, each confident in what he should be doing, with the presence of mind of where best to position himself, and having the passing and handling skills to accomplish what is best in the uncertain circumstances.

Apart from it being a delightful score, I also like the try because it highlights Welsh players' instinct and nous for the game; of belonging to them the inheritance of distant decades, of the rugby blood of generations coursing their veins.

Whilst admiring the try for exhibiting the attacking, maverick and mischievous essence of Welsh rugby, I have also the mixed feeling of regret.

The 1980s were a miserable time for Welsh rugby: it seemed to have come off the rails with nowhere to go. They were barren, forgettable days. The vision had blurred, the future opaque.

And yet here at Twickenham there was ample evidence that there were players around who could still show off and let the world know that gifted men were still alive in Wales and could run with the rest of the best the game had at that time to offer. Each of the players in that move was a brilliant player, a joy to watch playing joyous rugby. They lifted you up unawares from your seat, inspired by sweet unfettered emotion, to cheer loudly in celebration as well as in hope that some time soon it would all come well again. By the Noughties it did. We found our voice again. We could sing once more.

This try gives the sense of that.

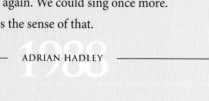

——————— ADRIAN HADLEY ———————

Adrian Hadley scores the first of his two tries against England at Twickenham in 1988. With arms outstretched, Mark Ring celebrates. Meanwhile England's Mick Skinner (no. 6) and Jon Webb are helpless.

(Colorsport/Colin Elsey)

Ieuan Evans: 'one of the great players of Wales'.

(Press Association)

IEUAN EVANS
v. SCOTLAND

National Stadium, Cardiff
20 February, 1988

'...he never allowed himself to fall into the mechanical kind of play and that blankness of mind which are the bane of the game. His nature was always alert, his spirits agile.'

Neville Cardus, of W.G. Grace.

'Scrum on the Scottish 10-metre line...'

... And so Bill McLaren begins his narrative on one of the best individual tries ever scored at what was then, and still is to those of a romantic, regretful, independent mood, the Arms Park.

'On the Scottish metre line... David Sole... David Young on this side... Now you notice...'

The master sporting wordsmith is about to explain the intricacies of front-row play but chuckles instead:

'The two flankers are having a private battle... Richie Collins and John Jeffrey,' who are indeed tugging at each other's elbows and jerseys away from the prying eyes of the referee who is on the narrow touchline side of the scrum, before the ball emerges from the scrum on the Welsh side.

Ieuan Evans sidesteps his way to an exhilarating try against Scotland at Cardiff in 1988.

(Colorsport)

'Jonathan Davies,' McLaren continues. 'Bleddyn Bowen… along the line to Ring… there's a chance here as Hadley's got it… pick up by Ring *(who has followed the ball around Hadley)*… Ieuan Evans. Evans all the way…Oh! What a blistering run….

'That is a magnificent try… Merlin the Magician couldn't have done it better… It was magic, magic all the way… What a score!'

And the Hawick stalwart is no less enthusiastic when the sequence is replayed:

'Just watch this … Jonathan Davies, Bowen … Then Ring … Watch how Ring picks up this low pass by Hadley … BRILLIANT…

'Then just watch what this man has to do … Ieuan Evans … Inside Hastings, inside Matt Duncan… Inside EVERYBODY … Jink, jink, jink…

'That was out of the top drawer…'

In a few scintillating seconds, and a great try, the talent of Evans is observed in all its glory, while the intricate plot is preserved magnificently in recollection by McLaren. He pieces together, first prosaically, the collective flow, no wasted words as the picture tells its own story. In an instant he brings to life – now more lyrically, with a mythical image – a famous rugby moment.

Ieuan Evans was a deadly finisher. Given the spare half yard, given an opponent's slight hesitation – or given nothing at all except his own skill and swiftness – he sniffed the wind and made the try line his rightful destination. At every stage during this run, Evans recognised his pathway, knew where he would end up: the postcode

'Merlin the Magician couldn't have done it better,' said Bill McLaren of Evans's solo effort and final lunge for the line past David Sole.

(Press Association)

of his destination was configured into his internal satellite navigation system. Three sidesteps later he had negotiated his way through a crowded defence, and a dive to avoid the final despairing tackle from David Sole gave Evans a try of mercurial, weaving virtuosity.

He had the pace of an athlete. He had the grace of a dancer, if I dare say as much of so rough and red-blooded sport. He could skim over the turf, hovering above the surface without his studs seeming to need to find any firm purchase in the pitch. With little sign of strenuous effort, he always seemed at ease with himself, as illustrated by his casual amble back after that score. He appears to swagger, feet splayed, posture erect and arms swinging. This, however, should not be interpreted as an arrogant strut. With a mischievous twinkle in his eye, and an engaging smile, it is, as he might say, his modest Carmarthenshire style.

Some seek to belittle opponents with a sidestep, which is fair game, as the slim, trim three-quarter longs to wreak revenge on the bulky bully. It is David's moment of subtle vengeance against the mighty Goliath of the game. Evans gives the impression that he simply seeks to show the joy that arises from exhibiting his talent for its own sake.

The south-east corner of the Arms Park, underneath the South Stand as it then was, with the try line at the Westgate Street end, could be said to belong to Ieuan Evans. In the late 1980s it was the stadium's only open end and it was there, where schoolboys gathered in their enclosure, that he carved for himself a piece of Welsh rugby immortality.

This was a difficult period for Welsh rugby. Jonathan Davies, disillusioned, went 'north'. Robert Jones, his scrum half, suffered too long behind a beaten pack of forwards. And the supporters saw precious little which chimed with the great tradition of the game in Wales. But the three daring tries scored by Ieuan Evans in that south-east corner evoked the heroic deeds of the past, briefly reasserting Wales's rugby identity

The first of these unforgettable tries was the one against Scotland in 1988. The second was scored against England in 1993 and it too has been Hallelujah-ed into legend: it gave Wales a victory, which was not only unanticipated beforehand, but also unlikely for most of the match itself.

That this defeat should have been inflicted on England, when the old enemy were playing for an unparalleled third Grand Slam, was interpreted as the sweetest of divine interventions on one side of Offa's Dyke, a cruel joke on the other.

Furthermore it was all the sweeter for Wales because they were the least likely of all the championship contenders to achieve as much. It also seemed like a fitting riposte to the England captain and management who, two years previously, had discourteously failed to attend the press conference after winning in Cardiff for the first time in 30 years.

'Daylight robbery': Ieuan Evans denies England victory at Cardiff in 1993.

(Press Association)

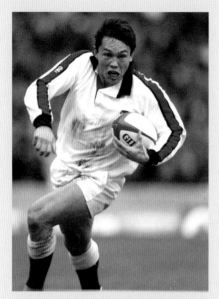

England's flying wing Rory Underwood was caught napping by Ieuan Evans in 1993.

(Press Association)

How the sequence of events began hardly matters. What lingers in the memory is the manner Evans seized the day. Evans, 5ft 10ins and 13 stone, went careering after the loose ball, punted up field by Emyr Lewis, once again more in hope than with deliberate intent. After all, with the way England were dominating proceedings, few chances were ever likely to come Wales's way.

Rory Underwood, the fastest winger in the world at the time, a most elegant runner and prolific try scorer, was Evans's opposite number. Evans needed to outrun him. Underwood, inexplicably, was caught napping on the turn. Evans was in full flight. Ahead there was Jonathan Webb – in a good position but on his own – to outwit. The English full-back hesitated and, with Evans in overdrive, it was no contest and all was lost for Webb.

The try was as dramatic as it was improbable. It was a sprinter's try. Its audacity either reduced spectators to silence or roused them

'Balancing precariously on the touchline,' Evans squeezes in at his favourite corner of Cardiff, against Ireland in 1993. (Press Association)

to thunderous applause and there was no doubting which side was which. But all agreed, because of England's obvious superiority on the day, that, unquestionably, it was daylight robbery.

The third of Ieuan Evans's great tries was also scored in 1993, but it was in a match which Wales lost to Ireland. This was of a different kind again. Emerging from a crowded space, and then balancing precariously on the touchline he maintained his balance and poise to run 30 metres and as the final lunging tackle came he squeezed inside the corner flag.

Unlike other great wings of his era – Underwood, Australia's David Campese, France's Patrice Lagisquet and New Zealand's John Kirwan, Evans seemed alert only when in motion. Casual, almost indifferent to all the furious commotion and seeming disorder around him, his mind seemed to be on other matters. Like Underwood and Lagisquet but unlike Campese and Kirwan, Evans had a genuine athlete's pace.

If all three tries delighted the eye with their style and panache, these recollections of Evans's extravagant gestures would not be complete without mention of a simple and very ordinary touchdown which held immense significance but was scored away from his beloved and exclusive patch of the Arms Park.

Evans described Campese as the most talented of his opponents, 'the first among equals'. In the third Test for the Lions in Australia in 1989, Campese fielding a ball on his own try line attempted, in his adventurous and maverick way, to run out of defence. Evans harried him into a mistake. Campese fumbled. Evans pounced on it to score the winning try. All very prosaic and ordinary, lacking the wonder attached to the others, but the try was significant nonetheless in that it paved the way to a Lions Test series victory in Australia.

The claims of greatness are frequently made these days on behalf of the merely modest among us, but Ieuan Evans is genuinely one of the great players of Wales. He was more than a local hero. His rugby gifts – subtlety and fine judgement rather than force and aggression – provided the keys to open the sternest of defences but also persuaded others to cross boundaries beyond parochial opinion.

He captained Wales on 28 occasions, played 72 times for Wales and scored 33 tries. To think of a sportsman as a wonderful ambassador might be an unnecessarily old-fashioned concept. Today sportsmen or women need only conform to the demands of their

sport and prove their worth only on the field of play. But this is a spurious idea. We need heroes.

His gesture, for instance, of delivering his after-dinner speech in French in Paris helped restore dignity at a time when Welsh rugby had much need of it after Wales had behaved badly whilst on tour in Australia in 1991 after losing 63–6. His 11-year career coincided with the leanest period in Welsh rugby history.

Welsh rugby felt that it needed something to boast about. As the master of deceptive flight on the field and with his honest, smiling dignity off it, in Ieuan Evans they had it.

1988 IEUAN EVANS

1989. Campese fumbles. Evans pounces. Lions win game. Aussies lose series.

(Colorsport/Andrew Cowie)

Jonathan Davies: 'maverick,
non-conformist, original...'

(Colorsport)

Try 11

JONATHAN DAVIES v. SCOTLAND

National Stadium, Cardiff
20 February, 1988

'Genius does what it must, talent does what it can.'

Owen Meredith, Earl of Lytton

'*Rwy wedi danto*,' sighed Jonathan Davies, disconsolately, shoulders stooped, head low, underneath the old North Stand of the old Arms Park. This was the tenth of December, 1988, and Wales had just played Romania. It would be nine years before he played for Wales again.

As team captain that day he was the last to leave as dusk descended. He had answered all the questions that the members of the media had showered on him, and chatted to all those who wished to hear his views on why Wales had just lost 9–15 to a fledgling rugby nation, the first time Romania had beaten away from their own country a team from what was then the Five Nations.

Translated, his words might mean that he was 'fed up', as well he might have been. But to put it so neatly is to understate his

*A meeting of mavericks: Jonathan Davies
and David Campese share a joke at Cardiff
in 1996.*

(Colorsport/Colin Elsey)

feelings, failing to encapsulate the weight and depth of emotion and frustration, bordering on resentment. Words can never fully describe deeply-felt emotions and in translation from Welsh into English the missing link remains doubly mistrusted.

There was a strong sense as he was making his crestfallen way, back to his hotel, of seriously blighted hopes. Here was a player who had beguiled and charmed us all now at the end of his tether, his promise and purpose extinguished. For a player who could introduce glamour to the bleakest Wednesday evening of rugby at the Gnoll in Neath or Stradey in Llanelli, he cut a forlorn and desolate figure.

'*Rwy wedi danto*'. The Welsh outside half's no. 10 jersey seems to bear the weight of a nation's passion and neurosis. So Davies understood and knew well the relentless bickering to come, the burden he would have to bear as captain of a losing team, more especially because he, on a pedestal, was such an attractive and compelling rugby player.

Only a few months earlier in the Five Nations Championship he had scored a try of scintillating beauty, of supreme confidence, nimble and clever, sure-footed and quick-witted, to outsmart a tight Scottish defence. For sheer audacity no other outside half at that time could have scored it. He was unique. He did things other players did not dare do or, if they did, only in their wildest dreams.

Earlier, he had taken a drop out on the 22-metre line: having shaped to kick in orthodox fashion where the forwards were lined up to his left near the touchline, he feinted to go one way then nudged the ball instead with the outside of his foot and ran away in the other direction. The scam completely hoodwinked the players, as well as the many million observers who had not seen anything of the kind before.

That Davies was capable of pulling a rabbit out of the bag was part of his stock-in-trade and you came to expect it of him, as you had of previous incumbents of that no. 10 jersey.

Wales has been blessed with the greatest of the rugby world's outside halves. They have scored wonderful individual tries. Cliff Morgan, my first international hero, scored a scintillating try on a heavy ground with straw piled high in the background against Scotland in Cardiff in 1956.

The mercurial Dai Watkins, whom I had greatly admired for his quick wits and swift running and with whom I was lucky to play,

A different league. Jonathan Davies about to score one of the great tries in either code of rugby, for Great Britain against Australia at Wembley in 1994.

(Colorsport)

was superbly off the mark in Dublin in 1964 to avoid the first line of defence and continued diagonally without an Irish hand touching him in Lansdowne Road.

Arwel Thomas received an unintentional tap back from Scotland's Tony Stanger at Murrayfield in 1997 to run 40 metres, with Welsh supporters holding their breath as he almost overran the dead-ball line.

Jonathan Davies's try is out of the same mould. His run is maverick, non-conformist, original in its conception; nothing so daring had been witnessed before in Cardiff. It was neat in its execution and taken in Davies's swashbuckling, impudent stride.

To begin with, self-evidently, he needed the ball to play with. In this he was, as he always had been, well served by Robert Jones at scrum half. The Trebanos-born player, was, to use a familiar Welsh adjective, 'tidy'. He was a beautiful passer of the ball, either to left or right; he had a low centre of gravity and was compact and sturdy. Though nuggety and combative, he was essentially a classical player, an elegant stylist. He was so correct. And I loved watching him.

Jones's competitiveness would come to the fore later with the Lions in Australia in 1989 when he disrupted the composure of the Australian scrum half and captain, Nick Farr Jones and was accused of stepping on the Wallaby's toes at a scrum in the second Test. It was a Test the Lions needed to win if, after losing the first, they were to stay to contest the series in the final match of the tour.

If there was the look of mischief on Jonathan Davies's face, a twinkle in the eye, and a confident swagger, Jones's demeanour suggested butter-not-melting-in-the-mouth innocence.

But 'There's no art to find the mind's construction in the face', and beneath the skin Robert Jones was as mischievous and competitive as his international half-back partner. He was a wonderful player. How puzzling later then that, after an almost immaculate performance by Jones at St Helen's, Swansea, the national coach of Wales at the time said that Jones 'had no place in his plans'. He wished for a player, in dimensions and inclinations, more akin, possibly, to the back row of the scrum.

Such coaches, it seems to me, must see the no. 9, and not the no. 10, as the fulcrum of the team. But, to my mind, the scrum half is the connecting link between backs and forwards, the servant of the outside half. His first priority is to ensure the swift, accurate delivery

The late Cliff Morgan, the author's first international hero. (Press Association)

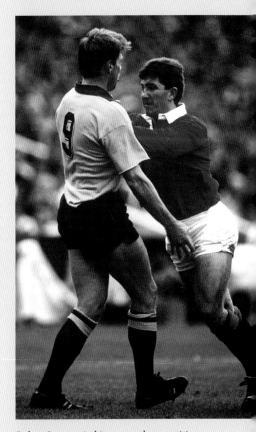

Robert Jones, mischievous and competitive, faces up to Nick Farr Jones in the second Lions Test in Australia in 1989.

(Colorsport/Andrew Cowie)

'There is a tiny gap which he sees…' Jonathan Davies cuts decisively inside Scotland's Gavin Hastings (no. 15) and Alan Tait at Cardiff in 1988.
(Colorsport)

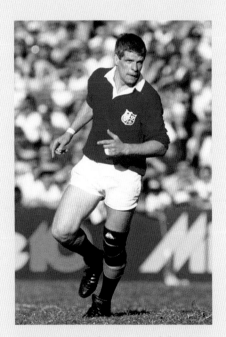

Scottish open-side flanker at Cardiff in 1988 was Finlay Calder, who would subsequently lead the Lions to victory against Australia in 1989.
(Colorsport)

of the ball into the hands of the man rightfully charged with the responsibility of determining the 'how', the 'where', the 'why', and the 'when' to play the game. And to give him the time to do so.

And on that February afternoon in 1988, it is Jones's reverse pass that makes things possible for Davies. A fourth back-row forward would not have had the wherewithal nor the agility and dexterity nor, dare I say, the selfless inclination to do so. The scrum halves of such heavyweight tendencies and slower responses have their leanings primarily towards themselves first – what's in it, what's on, for me – and onwards they charge.

No, without a player of Jones's intuition and his instinctive bond with the outside half, we would have been denied the joy of witnessing an undoubtedly great player on top of his game. Jonathan Davies was an original at a time when increasingly the drive and impetus was for uniformity and method. Davies could not, thankfully, be harnessed and fettered. He was no-one's marionette. And those who sought to deny him this freedom ultimately drove him to abandon rugby union in despair.

The try is a wonderful piece of instinctive play.

A scrum near Scotland's 22-metre line. The ball comes back quickly and uncontrolled, and Jones needs to recover his steps. He is facing the near touchline of the South Stand of the Arms Park. Forced to go that way and with no time to change direction to face his outside half, he flicks a long, high reverse pass to Davies, who needs to stop to gather the ball and to delay his run.

Such delay gives him time to assess the Scottish challengers. He comes inside the first on the scene, open-side flanker Finlay Calder and outside half Andrew Kerr. Davies, seeing his way blocked, taps the ball onwards. From then on it is a straightforward chase between him and no. 8 Derek White. Davies with an exceptional turn of pace gets there first.

I choose this one because of Davies's presence of mind, his quick thinking in a crowded space where nothing is on. The chances are that he is likely to be caught. There is a tiny gap which he sees. He chooses a grubber kick when, without the ball in his hands, no one can touch him.

Davies could not only cover the short distances which you would expect of an outside half but could run the length of the field too, as he showed later that season when Wales visited New Zealand and were overwhelmed by the All Blacks. In Auckland in the second of two Tests he ran some 60 metres to outpace the home team's defence for a spectacular try.

I always regretted seeing Jonathan Davies going north, to England and then Australia. I wanted to see more of his rugby genius, intuitive and independent, in the scarlet jersey of Wales.

JONATHAN DAVIES

Jonathan Davies, hammer of the Scots again, this time at Murrayfield in 1987. On his right are David Pickering and Paul Moriarty (with headband); on his left is John Devereux, and he is pursued by Scotland's David Sole and the blond-haired John Jeffrey. Beyond them are Davies's teammates Robert Norster (with headband) and Mark Jones.

Robert Howley: 'a world-class scrum half'.
(Colorsport)

Try 12

ROBERT HOWLEY
v. ENGLAND

National Stadium, Cardiff
15 March, 1997

'There must be a beginning to any great matter, but the continuing to the end until it is thoroughly finished yields the true glory.'

Sir Francis Drake

Robert Howley was an athlete at scrum half. But I had better explain myself more clearly.

Gareth Edwards, for instance, was not only a uniquely gifted footballer at school but also an outstanding athlete. I mean an 'athlete' in those precise terms: he competed on the track in athletics.

It is generally self-evident that in order to perform at the highest level in any sport a person needs to have the skills and the physical attributes essential to success in their chosen sport; to be prepared athletically. This does not mean that he or she necessarily has to execute what is expected of the 100-metre sprinter or the 400-metre hurdler, or which ever other athlete over which ever other distance of the track-and-field stadium. In another life and at another time, however, and before more specialized sporting times, Howley could have done so had he wished.

'A truly great finisher', Commonwealth Games athlete, J.J. Williams dives in at the corner to score against France at Cardiff in 1976.

(Press Association)

Olympic-hurdler-cum-try-scoring-wing Nigel Walker demonstrates his sprinting style to good effect as he strides in to score against France in Cardiff in 1994. Abdelatif Benazzi is, once again, left floundering.

(Press Association)

J.J. Williams actually did so. He was a sprinter on the track and, having retired from athletics, metamorphosed into a superlative wing for Wales in the 1970s, scoring some wonderful tries; a truly great finisher. This was true also of Nigel Walker, who from an Olympic hurdler evolved into a brilliant wing in the 1990s. This was at the turnaround stage when such accomplishments were still possible, though not in tandem. Like Williams and Walker, players would have to retire from full-time athletics first.

This dual capacity and achievement was always rare but possible, especially in days past when sport was largely amateur in both fact and in spirit. Football players, for example, who were paid but only minimally so, were free to pursue something different in the summer months. This is impossible nowadays. In rugby Ieuan Evans also had the pace and might have succeeded on the track and he, like Williams and Walker, was a winger.

Robert Howley, however, was a scrum half, and his athletic gifts were never ones necessarily required for those men who wore the no. 9 shirt. Whilst pace is always a vital factor in any position, it is judgement and presence of mind that is key at scrum half, as well as a good pass and, as I heard the male congregation loitering in judgement *outside* the chapel say somewhat puzzlingly, 'an educated boot'. And if the forwards were good enough and protective of the potentially more fragile colleague behind them, the scrum half might enjoy, so they opined, again somewhat perplexingly, an 'afternoon in an armchair'. For a ten-year-old, at the time, the game seemed full of riddles.

They might allow, grudgingly I admit, for a scrum half such as Onllwyn Brace (or 'David' as they complacently called him at Oxford University, where they might muster the necessary linguistic skills for French names, but not for Welsh ones) to be 'unorthodox' but, since no great case was made for it, he need not be equipped, apparently, with fleetness of foot.

Howley, on the other hand, could run. To watch him run was to see what a controlled style he had, arms and legs working in unison, elbows and knees functioning in tandem and not ill-aligned, as was so often the case with other players, whose knees pointed one way, elbows the other. Howley's shoulders held firm, his head steady, eyes direct and in this way he kept his good form.

Howley had proved himself a world-class scrum half after his first international against England in 1996, so much so that his opponents were promptly on red alert to make him a primary target. If they were to have a chance of success, they needed a plan not only to inhibit his freedom but to neutralise his force for mischief. He needed their full attention.

Half an eye might be thought enough to cast against the kind of scrum half who interprets his role as subordinate to his partner at outside half, a connecting link, a second fiddle. The flanker, in these circumstances, while remaining mindful, may not be too meticulous and may soon meander off elsewhere to make his own mark. Against a less menacing, more orthodox scrum half, he may feel he has time for second thoughts, to retrace his steps if needs be without any desperate consequences that might change the course of the game.

Having taken off 'like lightning', Robert Howley goes in at the corner against France in 1996.

(Press Association)

This could never have been the case with Howley. He was never in the habit of giving wing forwards a choice. They paid him their full attention.

He produced sufficient evidence from the second he first played to suggest that to ignore him for a moment was to risk a riposte of punishing and triumphant accuracy. When such a moment arrived, he invariably scored. In 1997 he scored six times in four pool games of the Heineken Cup for Cardiff (as they then were).

There was his unmistakable strength also. Though rugby was only in its second season as a professional sport, Howley was physically way ahead of other players of this time. Having shifted weights in training for some half a dozen years, his frame had the sharply defined contours of an extract from an Ordnance Survey map; the dips and rises were all in the right places and hugely formidable. Here was a player already fit for the modern game and what was expected of a professional player, with no floppy puppy fat.

'The physical dimensions are important,' he admitted, 'but are often lacking in Welsh players. Individual strength is vital in so competitive a sport.'

He could score from pure determination and strength, as he did against Wasps in the Heineken Cup, when close to the opposition line, he dived over and through a melee of players.

Others could emulate that feat, of course, but this was the first of two tries he scored that afternoon at the Arms Park. This kind of power alone is not in itself enough. It must be allied closely to other more clever and deceptive skills. To him belonged such legerdemain: with his sidestep and flourishing swerves he was capable of beating any man in a one-to-one confrontation. He had played a great deal of sevens rugby at school and later. This form of the game can fine tune the running and passing essentials of rugby and allow for an appreciation of what a man's talent is fully capable of and to encourage their display.

'There is so much space,' he once said. 'And if you succeed in taking players on and do so against faster men in the open field, then it gives you confidence to do so in 15-a-side.'

Speed off the mark played a vital role in many of his tries. Because of his speed and athletic agility, he played the role differently to anyone else playing in his position at his time in

Howley wins the Heineken Cup final for Wasps in 2004 as he touches a bobbling ball down right under Toulouse full-back Clement Poitrenaud's nose. Seven years earlier in Cardiff colours, he scored twice against the Wasps in the Heineken Cup

(Press Association)

rugby. And his second try against Wasps that day demonstrated this amply.

From behind a loose scrum of players near the halfway line, he read the moment and ran on the blind side. His sudden turn of pace took him beyond the first line of defence and into open field. The full-back to beat? With a shimmy he did so. To round off a spectacular run, he, athlete as he was, maintained his pace and power to cross the line. Other scrum halves might have accomplished the first two sections of this sequence but precious few, if any, scrum halves, would have polished off the third with such aplomb. He had an all-round ability other scrum halves did not possess.

Watching him cut a swathe through club defences was the wonderfully exciting sight of a player on the top of his eye-catching form, but to watch him in the international arena was even more beguiling theatre. Howley showed his gifts on several occasions.

*Robert Howley, alert and determined, finds a gap between England's
Will Greenwood (left) and Lawrence Dallaglio at Twickenham in 1998.*

'Wonderfully composed', Robert Howley flies through the air with the greatest of ease as he scores a spectacular long-range try in Paris in 2001.

(Press Association)

It is from here I would wish to choose a great try. But which one?

I have emphasised his authentic speed. His try against France in 1996 amply demonstrated this. With Nigel Davies caught by Thomas Castaignède in midfield on France's 22-metre line, Wales's attack is halted but the Llanelli centre just about hangs on to return the ball. Howley picks up and runs diagonally on the short side, straightens up 'to take off like lightning', says Bill McLaren: 'the pace of this man is something else'.

Paris also proved a happy hunting ground for him as he scored another star-studded try there in 2001. Scott Quinnell picks up at the back of the scrum within Wales's 22, charges beyond the first tackler before handing on to Howley. He is a long way out. The French left winger fails to touch him and is left floundering. Sadourny then confronts him. Gareth Thomas is outside for support if the scrum half needs it. A dummy confounds the French full-back and the try line beckons. Wonderfully composed, Howley scores.

In the same season he also outstripped England's defence on another long journey to the try line. These three tries were all scored during Wales's inglorious years. One statistic alone says as much. In seven matches between 1997 and 2003 (excluding the extraordinary Wembley fixture in 1999) England scored 303 points to Wales's 94.

Intoxicating as these Howley tries are, my choice from his treasure trove is his try against England in Cardiff in 1997.

It begins unpromisingly. Wayne Proctor is caught in midfield in his own half but, on his knees, he manages to get his pass away and so the movement continues. He finds Dale McIntosh on hand and to his left the back-row forward passes to Howley. Once more he sets out on his own. This time however there are men in his way, one sidestep and he upends one defender and onwards he goes. Then the second defender fares no better and grasps helplessly at thin air. Howley gathers himself for the final sprint for there is no other obstacle in his way and it is the line that lies ahead. It is a marvellous try.

On each of these occasions, Howley stood apart from the rest of his kind and to score tries to which we could exclaim: 'No other scrum half could have done that'. This was his sixth try for Wales. It is one of my favourites.

1997

——————— ROBERT HOWLEY ———————

Scott Gibbs: 'charging through straight and hard'.

(Colorsport)

Scott Gibbs
v. England

'Moments come to all of us when we are uplifted beyond
the ordinary; we become touched with grace for a while;
we become vessels of inspiration.'

Neville Cardus

Rugby inspires a variety of responses and emotions: sympathy and
affection; impatience and envy; fun and sullen silence. It is a bewitching
game of highs and lows which combines the bitter pill of defeat and the
sugary sweetness of triumph. But above all it is the unity of a shared
experience. It is the coming together for a brief moment, as the late Cliff
Morgan, quoting Jesse Owens, once put it 'to break bread at the same
table'.

Like other sports, it can surprise with its thrills and high jinks, and
can even allow occasional outbursts of fury born of irritation. It has also
its drama, but no melodrama, because, to the devoted follower of rugby
passion, its appeal is real enough.

Following your favourite sport is serious stuff. Though fun is central
to it, making fun of it is not. To the aficionado it is solemn business.

*'The day in Wembley is unforgettable'.
Try scorer Scott Gibbs, with loose-head
prop Peter Rogers on his back, leads the
celebrations as Wales secure an unlikely
victory over the Old Enemy in 1999.*

(Colorsport)

Yes, there is plenty of humour, but not at the expense of others. Sport, after all, must retain its ability to uplift, not diminish, the spirit; to share the camaraderie, not spoil it.

In rugby there are moments of sublime timing which divert what seems the game's natural and seemingly predictable course, and deny the favourite his moment of glory. The final, last-gasp try, say, deciding which of two equal sides succeeds in winning the game is in the natural course of a contest. It's not over, as they say, until the fat lady sings.

Less acknowledged are those more incongruous moments which refute all that has gone before, reducing one side to shocked silence, the other to unfettered, disbelieving joy. A player grows accustomed to losing a match if that's the way it has been for most of the game, but he is left desolate, seriously bereft, if defeat in these circumstances arrives only in the final seconds and against the run of play.

England understood this in April 1999. The compelling force of England's destiny that beautiful spring day had been well defined. Theirs had been an imperious march as they swept through the Five Nations Championship (Italy were to make it six nations the following season), and their grip on this final game, their crowning glory, was firmly established. England were on their way to the Grand Slam. The champagne should be prepared, as it might very well have been and nicely chilled, of course. And why not?

With Gibbs-like impact, Jamie Roberts scores in the final Lions Test in Australia in July 2013.

England had not only beaten Wales in recent years, they had trounced them. They had scored 34 points in Cardiff in 1997, 60 points a year later at Twickenham. Such was their supremacy at this time that they were, over the next five years to, score 209 points to Wales's 55. What happened in 1999 was a blip.

Wembley experienced a two-minute tumult of turmoil that day. Out of the blue came the touch of the magic arts.

This confounding of expectation is one of sport's eternal and veritable beauties. It is why we come back time and again to our seat in the stand. We want to be there to witness this.

But what of those whose hopes are dashed on such occasions? Defeat brings disappointment, suspicions of bad luck, frustration, sometimes anger too. These are to be expected.

With Wembley-like directness, Scott Gibbs takes the game to the All Blacks at Auckland in 1993. His fellow Lions are, left to right, Nick Popplewell, Peter Winterbottom and Rob Andrew. (Colorsport)

Neil Jenkins's eighth successful kick out of eight gives Wales their win at Wembley.

(Press Association)

The sense of despair was tangible on the man on the platform. There was no gracious acceptance of having been pipped at the post, no shrug of the shoulder and time to move on. No. Shuffling up and down at Reading station, he was desolate, his few words echoed a sense of thwarted hopes, of betrayal even, and the silence in between revealed how wretched the day had turned out. As yet, it was unlikely at this stage to get any better for him.

He was an England supporter dressed, dare I say, in the caricature of Twickenham man. Each of the nations has the cartoon stereotype to represent it: Wales has its cloth cap and muffler; Ireland the ginger-headed leprechaun; Scotland its tartan kilt and tam-o'-shanter. These are born of days gone by but resurrected when shorthand is required to denote the national character.

The man on the platform was looking down, as such phone-users do, at his ox-blood brogues and his salmon-pink corduroy trousers, while the evening chill was kept at bay by his waxed Barbour jacket. His trilby just about balanced on his head. Parading to and fro, swivelling now and again to retrace his steps, he was clearly agitated and speaking more loudly than was necessary, or wise. He was searching for the right words to explain everything. The prolonged train ride from Twickenham to Reading with its dozens of stops had added considerably to his dilemma and delay. There were the domestic commitments for the evening which he was clearly not going to honour. There were monosyllabic, acquiescent pledges. He was not going to make it in time, despite his earlier promises, to wherever his destination was meant to be.

Finally, since he was not able to convince his 'lady wife', he excused himself plaintively: 'Yes, yes, yes… but darling, we were robbed'.

It was the last throw of his desperate dice. The Chardonnay, which may well have flowed freely and sweetly during the day in the West car park, was soured at home; the soufflé ruined and on its rubbery, over-ripe way to the bin. There would be no soothing bird song for him in his idyllic Cotswold village. 'We were robbed…' But the guillotine waited.

I sympathised. I truly did.

What had happened at Wembley that day was an extraordinary turn of events. Another sporting rabbit was pulled out of the hat and, in a wink of an eye, everything changed. For one side, there was the brutal realisation that all was lost; for the other the lightning discovery that good fortune, at long last, had come their way. All the previous suffering and torment became in that incredible moment a matter of freakish laughter, not least because of that moment's unprepared-for, out-of-the-blue suddenness.

Max Boyce had defined such a thunderbolt many years before: it became known in the sporting lexicon as 'divine intervention'. There could be no better example of this than what happened on that beautifully sunlit afternoon in Wembley on 10 April 1999. It was Scott Gibbs's try against England.

Graham Henry, Wales's New Zealand coach, had been referred to as the Great Redeemer. For sure, or so it appeared, this victory was a revelation, a little miracle of sorts.

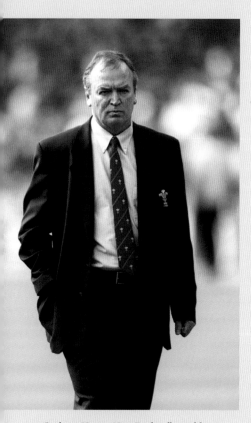

Graham Henry, New Zealand's world-cup-winning coach in 2011, Wales's Great Redeemer was very much the Strong Deliverer at Wembley in 1999. (Press Association)

This was the last fixture Wales played at Wembley, their temporary home since the National Stadium had been demolished to be replaced with a new stadium which had to be ready by the start of the Rugby World Cup later that year. Swivelled 90 degrees, the run of play and try lines henceforward in Cardiff would be North and South and not West and East as it had been during the old stadium's lifetime.

It is remarkable testimony to Wales's supporters' loyalty that English football's great stadium in London should be filled to capacity each time Wales played at the venue. Wales were encountering one of its very lean periods, yet still they travelled many hundreds of miles in their hordes from all corners of Wales to follow their team. Indeed Wembley proved a great success for two seasons.

The rugby played there seemed rubbed with stardust. Apart from its historical associations, Wembley gave a sense of expanse, and though he may not have the time, the player does have the space to swank. This may have been an illusion but all the rugby teams who played there during this period attempted to exploit the sense of freedom as if they felt the need in so hallowed a place to rise to the occasion.

Gwyn Jones, the former Wales captain, on his first visit to the stadium had written to say that he had played out his playground dreams of treading the famous turf. We have all been on that playground and we all understand the boyish glimpses of immortality. Jonny Wilkinson, at 19 the youngest on the field of dreams that day, wished that he might be back there again some day. The old Wembley was an iconic vision, since of all the world's sport stadia, Wembley was the most familiar to us.

Televised sport was in its infancy as we grew up in the 1950s and 1960s. The only certainty was that the FA Cup Final would always be on, just as the Rugby League Challenge Cup Final would be, both live from Wembley. There were no such guarantees of seeing rugby internationals from the Arms Park, Lansdowne Road, Murrayfield and Twickenham. They were not familiar in the way the Twin Towers were.

It is doubtful whether any other country could rely on such a

Jonny Wilkinson, England's world-cup-winner in 2003, kicks for goal at Wembley.

(Press Association)

The beautiful game… England's Tim Rodber (left), Wembley penalty culprit, joins with Neil Back in an attempt to inconvenience Scott Quinnell. Interested spectators behind them are Dafydd James and Scott Gibbs.

(Colorsport)

faithful band to follow a team of uncertain and often of threadbare quality. The M4, especially, was a busy and a bustling thoroughfare before and after the game, an overnight stay, say, at the famous Regent's Palace, no longer de rigueur since the motorway made the journey so much quicker than in days past.

Regrettably, London no longer exudes the same exciting carnival atmosphere which the other Six Nations cities nowadays still enjoy.

In days past the prelude to the match included a man in a white suit with a baton standing high on a podium on the pitch conducting the community singing, ending with 'Abide With Me'. This now is as nostalgically redolent of days gone by as the cockerel emerging in the laurel wreath cockadoodledooing to announce *The Pathe News* in the cinema. Which is where you were likely to get pictures of international rugby matches, as I remember.

In contrast the sunny spring day on 12 April had begun with Tom Jones and Max Boyce providing the pre-match entertainment.

There was a sneaking feeling that with two such top-class entertainers headlining the day, that the match that was to follow might fall far short of the feel-good factor provided by the show business style of Jones and Boyce. Would the game prove to be an anti-climax after the throbbing rhythms? Wales had lost to Scotland and Ireland but had won a terrific match in Paris against France. But we were to be well rewarded: the spectacle's beginning would be well matched by the extravaganza at the end.

England were going for the Grand Slam, as they had been doing in the previous seasons, 1996, 1997 and 1998. In these three years only France could halt the English juggernaut, and they did. If Wales and France were the usual title-chasers in the 1970s, by the century's closing years England had superseded Wales. Welsh rugby had seen better days.

Instead of building on the good days and using the strong and highly evocative tradition, there arose a strange suspicion of the successful times. Recalling the 1970s became an anathema.

Scott Gibbs's try with 90 seconds of extra time already played was an intervention of phenomenal status. If so then England themselves had played their own part in their downfall. They had scored three tries in the first half to give them a 25–18 lead with Wales staying close only through Neil Jenkins's immaculate kicking. England also made incorrect judgements as well as mistakes. Two crucial ones led to Wales surviving to find the chance to win.

Critically, with seven minutes to go, England, given a penalty 36 metres out, chose to go for a line-out rather than allow Jonny Wilkinson to go for goal. Success with this kick would have given England a nine-point lead, two scores ahead, and the door would have surely been shut on Wales. Then Tim Rodber was adjudged illegally to have shoulder-charged Colin Charvis. From this penalty Wales gained the territory from which Gibbs's try was scored.

From a line-out Chris Wyatt leapt high to tap the ball down to Howley, to Scott Quinnell. The no. 8's pass was short for Gibbs to come charging through straight and hard. He went on beyond four defenders to score. The roar from the 78,000 crowd was tumultuous and deafening. But the try was not enough. The conversion is what would bring the victory. Jenkins, as he had so often done, ensured that he did so. He succeeded with eight kicks out of eight on this occasion, indicating as he did in South Africa with the Lions, the strength of his temperament under pressure. The crowd for the second time gave a hair-raising roar.

The drama of Gibbs's try, coming as late as it did, in a game in which Wales were never in the lead until the second minute of injury time, was uniquely memorable. It was great theatre in the truest sense, infused with humour, not at England's expense, even if some may have thought so but because the light-fingered fraud had been so outrageously unbelievable. The unforeseeable had come so prodigiously to pass and England fell from grace. The day in Wembley is unforgettable.

The man at Reading station had every right to believe that England had been robbed.

SCOTT GIBBS

1999

'Songs of praises I will ever give to thee...' Scott Gibbs scores, watched by a slightly amused touch judge and a slightly less amused Martin Johnson.
(Press Association)

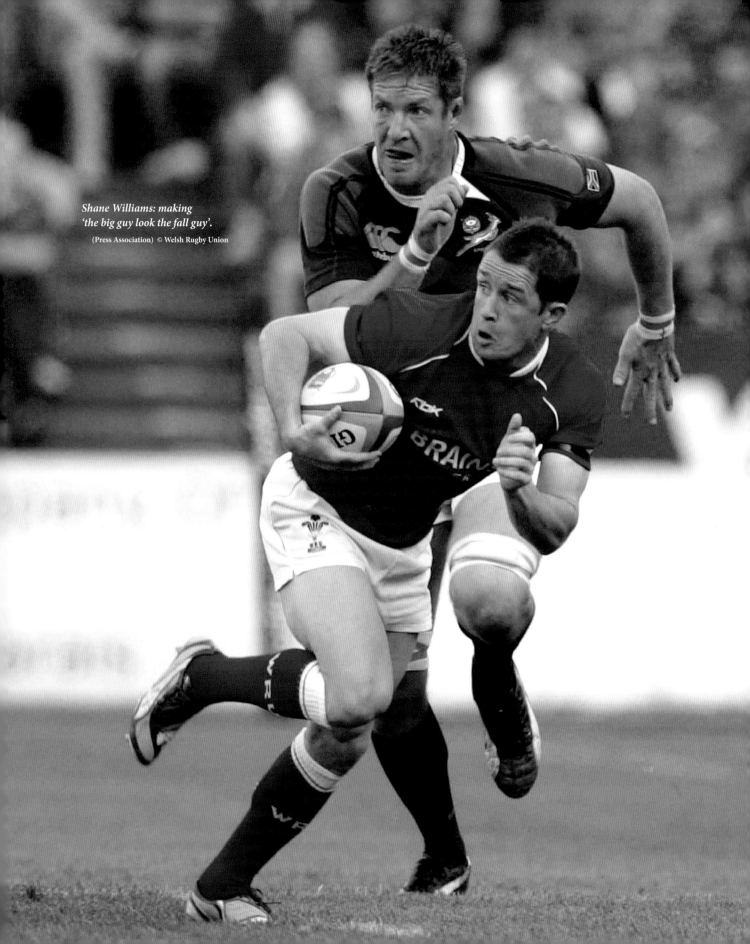

*Shane Williams: making
'the big guy look the fall guy'.*

(Press Association) © Welsh Rugby Union

Try 14

SHANE WILLIAMS
v. SOUTH AFRICA

Loftus Versfeld, Pretoria
14 June, 2008

'See, the conquering hero comes!
Sound the trumpets, beat the drums!'

'Joshua', Thomas Morrell

In the 21st century, Shane Williams came to claim his kingdom.

Wales had grown short of heroes on the rugby field, such heroes as the world universally came to recognise, lauded and honoured. There had unquestionably been very great and famous players during Wales's barren period throughout the 1980s and 1990s and there had been individual games when their stars were able to shine brightly in the firmament, among them Jonathan Davies, Robert Jones, Ieuan Evans, Scott Quinnell, Gareth Thomas and Mark Taylor, who all scored great tries. But, sadly, there were no consistent performances by the team as a whole; an occasional win here and there was a slim diet.

And what of others who were truly among the elite, like Bleddyn Bowen, Mark Ring, Robert Norster, Gareth Davies and Terry Holmes? We were given but rare glimpses of their refined play and agile minds,

and they were forced to play a solitary game, because the teams
they belonged to were short of the first rate and lacked an overall
championship quality. With better guidance perhaps there might have
been more who would have reached the top flight.

There was a good deal of frustration about and a sense of ambition
thwarted. The rugby mood was soured in Wales, as reflected by the
sense of personal defeat, betrayal even, in Jonathan Davies's departing
words: *'Rwy wedi danto…'* He had left Wales to play rugby league.
He wasn't the first or last, indeed the player drain in those years was
significant.

*'Forced to play a solitary role'. Terry Holmes,
playing for Wales against New Zealand in
1978, was one of those great players who
found himself all too often in teams which
struggled on the big stage.*

(Colorsport)

Going for broke at Croke in 2008. Ireland's Andrew Trimble (no. 12) and Tommy Bowe (11) are left in a heap as Williams scores a crucial try, watched by Tom Shanklin.

(Colorsport/Kieran Galvin)

Here is the long list of the departed:

1986	Robert Ackerman, Gary Pearce
1987	David Bishop, Adrian Hadley
1989	Jonathan Davies, Paul Moriarty, Jonathan Griffiths, John Devereux
1990	David Young
1991	Mark Jones, Rowland Phillips, Kevin Ellis, Allan Bateman, Gerald Cordle
1991	Matthew Silva
1993	Richard Webster, Scott Gibbs
1994	Scott Quinnell

Not all of these, admittedly, were in the top rank. But, not only was the road 'north' paved with gold (there were generous signing-on fees), it seemed to lead to something that was better than the sullen mood that permeated Welsh rugby. Wales was no longer a land fit for rugby heroes.

Wales also lacked at this time a significant and influential leader who could promote a collective feeling of pride, of sporting responsibility and to promote a sense of purpose. Wales needed a strong personality to show the way.

In 1995 the rugby union world changed. If in 1888 Robert Seddon and his troupe of 22 players went on the first tour of Australia and New Zealand as what later became known as the British and Irish Lions, and were paid £200 each for the 54 matches they played over an eight-month period, rugby union had remained resolutely amateur for the next 107 years. In Paris in 1995, Vernon Pugh, the Chairman of the International Rugby Board, declared the game 'open' signalling the game's professional status henceforward. The flow north was forever dammed, the reservoir of Welsh rugby union talent could be held back. Until, that is, the players were enticed to the vasty fields of France or by the wealthier club owners in England. The exploitation of Wales's abundant pool continued, it was just that the poachers were new.

Shane Williams was home grown in the Amman valley and never left during his bright days in the sun. He was the kind of player Wales yearns to court in the national jersey and longs to cherish. He strutted with pent-up energy on the left wing. Sometimes he seemed unobtrusive, moving softly and stealthily like a cat in and around the furniture with careful steps. Then when there was a glint and a glimmer of movement which caught his eye, he would spring into fluent and well balanced action, nimble and neat.

What elevates him also and gives immense pleasure is that he cuts across the modern mood of an increasingly physical sport which encourages muscular men to charge forever, as if drawn magnetically, to midfield collisions; not to avoid but to aim for a head-on impact.

Williams instead glided over the open green, a will-o'-the-wisp, a haunter and a hunter. For Wales and the Ospreys, he deferred to no pattern, obeying only his whim and, who knows, the bidding of fear. He looked not to confront and to intimidate with bruising shoulders but rather, with seeming innocence and a rebel sense of mischief, to search for the spaces in between the defensive brick blocks. Opponents feared this spectre, lest he embarrass them with his mesmerising running and jinking.

After the lean years everybody in Wales had hoped for a breath of fresh air. They longed for someone different who would break the mould of the heavyweights. Williams did so, royally providing for our dreams.

Rugby union's authorities are always at pains to emphasise those enduring qualities that have from the very beginning been attached to their game. Who would disagree that rugby should remain a game of all shapes and sizes? With the game having embraced professionalism in 1995, with more time devoted to training and overall fitness and the resultant change in body shapes, this claim – this hope – may be under threat.

It remains rugby's perennial joy for the small man, the whippersnapper with wings in his heels, to make nincompoops of the bigger men; it is the dramatic light and shade of the seemingly unequal struggle. From his very first cap against Italy, Williams held a candle to show the way for the value of this difference and he came out on top when forces railed against him.

Like the young boy on his first day at school, looking fresh faced and tidy, in a uniform he has yet to grow into, Williams appeared to rub shoulders with the usual overbearing suspects from the sixth form, who wanted to throw their weight about and show who's boss. For instance Italy chose Cristian Stoica at 6ft 2in and 15st 10lb to carry out the role of the schoolyard bully. He did not get away with it.

Williams at 5ft 8in and 13st 4lb was meant to have no chance against such a man, in much the same way as Christophe Dominici of France, another lightweight, was perceived to be a throwback to a more fanciful and idealistic age. The Frenchman was thought to be no match for the All Blacks but his moment arrived gloriously and triumphantly in the 1999 Rugby World Cup semi-final. The small man found his stage, established his credentials and condemned pre-judgement to the dustbin.

This prejudice had worked against Williams. Neither Graham Henry nor his successor Steve Hansen favoured him initially. Having been capped in 2000, he was not to appear again until 2003. His return to favour came in the world cup in Australia, where, late in the tournament, after having been excluded for the first three matches in Pool D, he was reinstated in the final game of the round against New Zealand and then for the quarter final against England. Cocking a very definite snook at the prejudice that had kept him out of the Welsh team, Williams played with panache and influence.

France's Christophe Dominici, like Shane Williams, a lightweight 'throwback to a more fanciful, idealistic age'. (Press Association)

It says a great deal about Shane's strength of character that he was not cowed by this arrant neglect.

Both these New Zealand coaches, insensitive to the incorrigible and mercurial Celtic temperament, should have blushed with embarrassment at the error of their judgement. Williams's effervescence and running adventure were unstoppable in both games and, as with every match thereafter, the ball reaching his hands prompted a thrilling sense of expectancy.

From the very distant past, from the days of Arthur Gould, Gwyn Nicholls and Dickie Owen at the beginning of the last century, people have gone to watch rugby not necessarily to watch the team play, nor necessarily for the score, but rather to watch a favourite player strut his stuff. To see him alone is worth the price of a ticket.

Shane Williams lit up every game he played. He was a fine taker of the slimmest chance, able, with an intake of breath, to change direction at will as he did against Italy in 2008; or he knows when the straight line is the better alternative as he did so thrillingly against Scotland in the same year. Indeed, if it can be said of so full a rugby career, 2008 was his *annus mirabilis* with six tries in the Championship.

Unlike other intrepid adventurers, he seemed always to be in control; his head always knew what his feet were up to. Even if sometimes he took a risk too far and was brought down with bruising force. Yet he rarely needed the attention of the 'magic sponge'. No one needed to worry. It was he, after all, who could make the big guy look the fall guy.

Williams had that irrepressible flair which is irresistible to the Welsh, who might admire the tough side of rugby but enjoy the clever play more. In his sidestep, his speed off the mark, his balance and control, you sensed mischief.

If he had been of another age, he might have been in tune with the anarchy of rock n' roll, his body gyrating to a loose and maverick rhythm not a conforming, repetitive rehash of what had gone before. Unlike the hip-swivelling rock 'n rollers, however, who (purportedly)

Shane Williams gliding 'supremely, almost contemptuously, away' to score against South Africa at Loftus Versfeld, Pretoria in 2008.

(Press Association)

excited young girls to declining morals, Shane with his cherubic face and engaging smile, seemed the kind of boy mothers would gladly invite to Sunday tea to meet their daughters. The fathers, in the meantime, inspired by him would secretly in their high-backed winged chair imagine themselves back in their salad days playing like Shane Williams.

I remember my first sight of him.

Not long into his brief tenure as coach to the Wales team, Graham Henry invited 98 players to St Helen's, Swansea. There were to be two trial matches to determine what the future had in store for Wales's national game. It was a tall order. To assist him in this exercise he conscripted the help of 19 former Welsh international players to advise him and to make suggestions. I was there to view the wingers.

It appeared at the time to be a significant moment. Former players had, by and large, been ignored and it looked as if an outsider was hinting that this ought to change. Welsh rugby had been going through troubled times, and, with no signs of imminent international success, a state of permanent decay threatened.

The second time I saw Shane was a couple of days later at the Vale resort where Henry had also invited the former internationals for dinner in the evening and to share a table with those players we had been invited to study. It was that evening I had occasion to talk to him and Gareth Thomas. Later that week I dropped them both a line, wishing them well and hoped that they would achieve, in time, what they both, in their contrasting styles and shapes, wished for themselves. It appears that they have done so.

For me, there lies a major dilemma, however. Williams scored many good-looking tries, but which one to choose?

There is the try against Argentina in 2004 where, on his way to the line, he jinked one way and then, within a stride or two, seamlessly in the other direction to score under the post. Another favourite was against Ireland at Croke Park, Dublin, where with the game in the balance and with little room to manoeuvre, he used his pace and deceptiveness to avoid the defence to dive over in the right-hand corner. This was not dissimilar to the try against Scotland in 2008 where on the narrow corridor along the touchline he outstripped the Scottish defence to dive over with barely daylight between him and the corner post.

Dwayne and Shane and Alfie shout! Messrs Peel, Williams and Thomas celebrate the 2005 win over England at Cardiff.

(Press Association) © Welsh Rugby Union

'With barely daylight between him and the corner post', Shane Williams is about to squeeze in at the corner in spite of Scotland's Nikki Walker's efforts.

(David Davies/PA Wire) © Welsh Rugby Union

I suppose the one I would choose on a very crowded list is the one he scored in the second Test in South Africa where the contest between him and Bryan Habana was at its height. It is the second try in the second Test where he picks up a loose ball and outpaces Smit, the South African hooker. Then, with five other Springboks converging to force him into the corner, he sidesteps inwards, halts the advancing horde and then, as they hesitate, he sidesteps out again and glides supremely, almost contemptuously, away. He had that crucial ability: having sidestepped one way, he could change direction and sidestep the other.

He had done something similar against Argentina in 2004 in Buenos Aires. I was lucky to be present at both matches.

2008

SHANE WILLIAMS

'Yeeeeeees!' Shane Williams's last try for Wales, scored in his last match for Wales, against Australia in Cardiff in 2011. His shirt says simply 'Diolch', the Welsh word for 'thanks'.

(Press Association) © Welsh Rugby Union

Gareth Edwards: scorer of Wales's greatest individual try ever.

(Press Association)

Try 15

GARETH EDWARDS *v.* SCOTLAND

National Stadium, Cardiff
5 February, 1972

'They ought to build a bloody cathedral on the spot.'

Spike Milligan

Ask the mastermind of the brains trust at the 'four ale' bar about Gareth Edwards and he will fulminate about the greatest try ever scored: Gareth's, for the Barbarians against the New Zealand All Blacks in January 1973 at Cardiff Arms Park. (He will spell all this out in full, including the name of the old ground to which he is particularly partial, to lend a modicum of accuracy to his tale). He was there, he will say. Along with the many million others.

Just as is the case with Stradey Park and Llanelli's famous victory over the All Blacks in 1972, Cardiff Arms Park was utterly inadequate to accommodate everyone who nowadays claims that they were there. The sequence has been shown so often that it has become part of our rugby lives, and it is easy to believe that we were all there. Who would dare, macho men all, admit one's absence from rugby's most glamorous

and solemnised team moments? But it was also the coronation of a
rugby eminence, a great player, a nonpareil. The throne was Gareth
Edwards's.

Others will draw attention to the try he scored against Scotland
in the Five Nations Championship the previous season. Or the one
against France at Stade Colombes in Paris in the drawn match in 1969
when sheer strength and, he would claim, his gymnastic ability fused
together for the try. Whatever was responsible for his score, he took
several desperate French players along with him, each claiming any
spare part of him or his jersey they could to get hold of, as he dragged
himself, broad-shouldered, barrel-chested over the line, with Pierre
Villepreux the last to cling on to him.

These were, of course, undeniably great tries but were unexpected
and played on the hazard. Who would have imagined them? They
belonged to the school yard perhaps, where imagination could run
wild and without limits when, with poetic fancy, Wales always won
against impossible odds, heroically with tries of dramatic invention,
after suffering despair and scraped knees, and triumphing invariably in
the dying seconds.

These tries are born of that unconfined childhood mystique and
liberation; a kind of rhapsody of the ideal kind which seems so natural

in youth. When such tries are scored, we feel once more the loosening of the ties of straitlaced and bridled adulthood. This is rugby as we wish it to be.

This is rugby beyond the strictures and common sense of any coaching manual, dry and practical, where every metre is measured, where every position of the elbow matters, every space covered, every gap closed and every attacking player imprisoned, with its instinct for the 'can't do' rather than the speculative 'can do'.

These tries are rugby with a free spirit.

For Spike Milligan there was certainly more than harmony that entranced him. There was another vision that came to him, another-worldy realm to which he was transported.

In these instances the opposition defence was not ready and waiting: like everyone else, it was taken by surprise. It is the genius of the player to see the chance and to seize the moment for his own. It belongs to him and has come to belong to him alone. Such moments, repeatedly, are recollected in celebration and, even now, they manage to retain their sense of novelty and innovation and are recited with equal excitement and enthusiasm as if newly minted.

Gar and Ger. Gareth Edwards passes to his Welsh teammate, the author, at Cardiff in 1972 under the beady eyes of, from the left, the All Blacks Keith Murdoch, Grant Batty (no. 11), Ian Kirkpatrick and Sid Going. In support, as ever, is Dai Morris.

(Colorpsort/Colin Elsey)

Sheer strength and gymnastic ability took Gareth Edwards to a succession of tries, this one against England at Cardiff in 1976. Mike Lampkowski is his hapless opposite number.

(Colorsport)

However, there were also the tries he scored from close to the line, where defences were seemingly well-organised and well-prepared. They knew *what* was coming. They also knew *who* was coming. They knew, too, the likelihood of *how* it was coming.

We've been here before, they might ponder as they settled in the game's static moments at the scrum or line-out. However vigilant their purpose, they might also have felt at the back of their minds a slight hesitation, a brittle flaw, that they were doomed to fail, that what was to come was inevitable. And 'come' it invariably did. Thus, with the remnants of a failed strategic barricade helpless in his wake, they were forced to sup from their cup of sorrows, with which vintage they were, by now, all too familiar.

Whoever the man or woman and whatever the sporting conquest may be, the enduring image of a player may be etched in the mind's eye, preserved forever as if in aspic, by a single outstanding moment. All their other achievements, however supreme, will be encapsulated in one timeless frame. Whatever has gone before and whatever is likely to come thereafter, one transcendent flash and momentary wink of their masterly stuff will remain suspended, when all else will drift among the mists to be recalled only in some deeper, more detailed debate long into the intoxicated night.

This in no way diminishes them. Rather it becomes the signature of their many achievements. It is what seals, the contract between them and their own talent, and between them and their public.

Think of Stanley Matthews in the 1953 Cup Final; Roger Bannister's run at Iffley Road in1954; Lynn Davies's leap in Tokyo 1964; George Best's solo goal for Manchester United against Benfica in 1968; Gordon Banks's save in the 1970 Mexico World Cup against Brazil; Mike Gibson's sportsmanship for Ireland signalling Barry John's drop goal for Wales; Mary Peters's Olympic smile in Munich 1972; Willie John McBride lifted aloft in Johannesburg in 1974; Fran Cotton embalmed in mud in the photograph by Colin Elsey in New Zealand in 1977; Andy Irvine against France in 1980; Ian Botham's unbeaten 149 against Australia at Headingley in 1981; Torvill and Dean's 'Bolero' in 1984; Sebastian Coe crossing the line in the 1500 metres at the Moscow Olympics of 1984, and Steve Ovett stealing the 800 metres in the same Games; Ryan Giggs's goal against Arsenal in the FA Cup semi-final replay in 1999; Tanni Grey in the 1994 London Marathon; Nicole Cooke coming up the slope, round the bend in the rain on her cycle ride to the Olympic gold in 2008.

This random personal list can so easily be extended and be updated by a different generation.

Gareth Edwards is, however, fixed by two such iconic moments. Yes, there is Gareth the Barbarian and that elegant dive through the air to the exultant strain of Cliff Morgan's 'Oh, that fellow Edwards'.

But there is a second moment, another try, a triumph of stamina and control. It is the ineradicable memory of the uninterrupted long run to score against Scotland at Cardiff in 1972. But it is also, and more so possibly, the vision of an ochre-matted figure returning from the race to the line after lying on the greyhound track that surrounded the pitch at the Arms Park in those days. From head to toe he is besmirched with the mud of the track as he dived over ahead of the despairing clutches of what is left of the beleaguered Scottish defence. The television cameras emphatically capture the enduring image, testimony to the prodigious, breathless effort that forged the remarkable try.

After wondering whether Gareth would score, McLaren, suggested that it would be 'a miracle if he could'. And he does.

George Best. The name is enough. (Press Association)

Another Manchester United legend, Ryan Giggs, on his way to scoring one of the greatest individual goals ever, against Arsenal in 1999.

(Press Association)

Ian Botham smashes the Australians all around Headingley in 1981.

(Colorsport/Stewart Fraser)

Sebastian Coe wins Olympic 1500-metre gold at Moscow in 1980.

(Press Association)

'You can read on his face,' observes McLaren as he watches the dirt-encrusted hero return triumphantly to the exultant cacophony, 'the effort, the power, the strength, the fitness that took him there.'

Since Biblical references abound, it would not have been out of place for the Hallelujah chorus to strike up.

The sequence began with a line-out for Scotland deep in Welsh territory. Peter Brown gets his hands to the ball at the back of the line, but he does not secure a firm hold which allows Mervyn Davies to steal it. A maul forms, from which the ball emerges so swiftly that Roger Arneil, the Scottish flank forward, has no time to recover lost ground. As Gareth first gets his hands on the ball and begins his run, he fends off an off-balance Arneil.

Gareth is now in free space. He crosses his own ten-yard line. He steals a glance to his right. As he does so, you are drawn to his eagle-eyed awareness, taking a peep at what's available but coming to terms with the fact that he is a Welshman out on his own, alone, and that it is now or never.

Until I heard his television interview with David Parry Jones of BBC Wales who prompted Gareth to add his own words to the try and give his thoughts, I believed he had been looking for me. I was not there. There are those who thought I should have been on his shoulder. But since it had been Scotland's throw-in at the line-out, I had, as was my style, retreated to cover the 'box' kick, in other words, that unoccupied area for the defending team behind the line-out. With the full-back in midfield, it is wide open to be exploited.

Positioning myself there also meant that I was able to cover behind my own three-quarter line in the event of the opposition deciding to move the ball wide among the backs.

With Gareth out of the blocks like whippet, it took me some time to recover from being back on my defensive heels to being on my toes in attack. The distance between us had opened up. At least I got to him first after his touchdown, although I'm not sure whether he welcomed such close attention so soon after his lung-bursting chase. Whether he was pondering the magnitude of what he had achieved or whether he was simply – what's the word— knackered, I have yet to ask him. At any rate while he was lying outstretched, 'the sheer magic...' according to McLaren of what had been witnessed, 'had brought the whole stadium to its feet.'

What makes this outstanding, in the truest sense of that word, is that it was a scrum half who scored it. We could not have imagined a player from this position running so far and lasting the pace. That kind of running might have been expected of other players in the other positions among the back division, but not from scrum halves. No one within memory had done so before, no Wallaby or Springbok or All Black, even. None could have matched his powerful endeavours or his all-round athleticism. Robert Howley was to come for Wales. But the prototype has not been surpassed. His achievements were glorious.

What Ian Wooldridge wrote of a Ted Dexter innings applies to Gareth's exploits : 'It was the manner of their making that transformed his deeds into the dream of all schoolboys and the fireside romance of old men.'

And the try he scored at Cardiff that day remains the best Welsh try I've ever seen.

1972

GARETH EDWARDS

'None could have matched his powerful endeavours or his all-round athleticism'.
Gareth Edwards's last try for Wales, in his last match for Wales, against Scotland
at Cardiff in 1978. His Scottish opponents are, from left to right, Alastair Cranston,
Jim Renwick and Donald MacDonald. Gazing admiringly on is the author.

(Colorsport/Colin Elsey)